TEAMS
THAT
SELL

SET, BUILD & MANAGE
HIGH PERFORMING TEAMS
IN THE NEW ERA OF B2B

Martin Nyrong Mortensen
Thomas Barre &
Sixten Schultz

Spintype

MARTIN NYVANG MARIUSSEN
THOMAS BØRVE &
SIXTEN SCHULTZ

TEAMS THAT SELL

spintype

Teams That Sell lays out a blueprint for how commercial leaders organize around one of the main developments we saw during my time at Sales Performance International and are still seeing today. The need for greater collaboration to succeed with sales. Selling is growing in complexity and difficult things are better solved by working together than working alone".

Jürgen Heyman

Former CEO & Executive Chairman Sales Performance International (SPI)

Teams That Sell
– Set, Build & Manage High Performing Teams in the New Era of B2B
1. Edition 2023
Copyright © 2023 The Authors & Spintype

Authors: Martin Nyvang Mariussen, Thomas Børve & Sixten Schultz
Book layout: Spintype.com
Cover design: Per-Ole Lind
Printed by: AKA Print A/S
Published with: Spintype.com
Proofreader: ProofReadingPal

ISBN print: 9788771921489
ISBN pdf: 9788771921496
ISBN epub: 9788771921502

CONTENTS

ABOUT THIS BOOK

- Simple tasks are best solved by individuals and complex ones are better solved by teams of people with complementary skills working together.

This book is about how business leaders grow sales, efficiency, foster employee engagement and create a better customer experience, by creating *Teams That Sell* rather than *teams of individual sales reps* for a business-to-business environment that is becoming increasingly complex to sell in.

- Why does business-to-business selling need to move from being managed by sales individuals to *Teams That Sell* as business-to-business selling grows in complexity?

- What type of *Teams That Sell* should be set up for different types of selling?

- What will make the transformation successful?

At Kvadrant Consulting, our team has spent decades helping business leaders and commercial executives make sure that their sales and marketing organizations are set up to succeed in a constantly changing buying and selling environment.

Although we have done our fair share of salesforce development projects over the years for many different types of clients across different industries, we offer *Teams That Sell* now because of a fundamental shift happening in how we optimize the salesforce through how we organize it.

From recommendations that would previously highlight how companies could get individual salespeople to sell more effectively, to recommendations that would instead highlight the potential value of getting teams of people, with complementary capabilities, to collaborate around selling.

Turn the challenges of change into opportunities for value creation.

This shift in how we look at salesforce optimization—from optimizing at the sales individual level to optimizing at the team level—did not appear out of the blue. Rather, it is the product of the many changes in business-to-business sales that have taken place over the past decades that have made it increasingly more appealing to make selling a team effort conducted not only by traditional salespeople.

- **The external environment that salespeople operate in is becoming more complex:**
  More people involved in the average purchase, a "messier" sales process where buyers loop back and forth, better-educated buyers that allocate less time to vendor salespeople and use more channels to engage with vendors.

- **The internal company environment that salespeople operate in is becoming more complex:**
  Company products are becoming more complex with higher frequency of new offering launches, greater requirements for collaboration with other functions like marketing, growing requirements to use new sales enabling technology and data for smart decision-making.

This book is about those changes, and about how sales leaders turn the challenges of change into opportunities for value creation.

THE CRITICAL CHOICE FOR SALES LEADERS ABOUT THE FUTURE OF THEIR SALES ORGANIZATION

As business-to-business selling changes, sales leaders are left with a choice on how best to manage this growing complexity:

- Keep piling on new requirements at the level of each sales individual, teaching them how to do thought leadership, social selling, and hybrid selling; how to be a mini-marketer; and how to use sales enablement platforms, CRM systems, CRM system add-ons, and automations

Or:

- Create sales teams that can manage the new requirements at a collective level

Complex challenges (such as selling in the new buying environment) are more effectively managed by a team of people with complementary capabilities, rather than individuals with the same capabilities who are asked to do everything by themselves. For this reason, *Teams That Sell* are becoming the preferred way forward for commercial leaders looking to improve the performance of their organization.

> ## Make the sales organization a better place to work.

One study of 21,392 sales opportunities[1] found that the win rates on those with multiple people involved in the sales process was 258% higher compared to those with only one person involved.

---

1. https://www.gong.io/blog/team-selling/

But for the organizations we work with, it is not only about hard sales efficiency and effectiveness metrics.

It is equally about creating great places to work for people in the sales organization who are engaged and enthusiastic about their job and the work that they do.

The case for *Teams That Sell* as an enabler of this is clear.

Only 8% of people not working on teams are engaged in their work; however, that number increases nearly five-fold to 45%, for people working in teams with a team leader they trust.

Teams That Sell not only illustrates the most effective way to manage the growing complexity of selling, it also provides ways to make the sales organization a better place to work, with people who are fully engaged in their work.

This book is not only about how commercial leaders grow sales efficiency and effectiveness, but also about how to create a sales organization where people love to work.

FOCUS ON HELPING SALES LEADERS ANSWER 4 CRITICAL QUESTIONS

The book deals with four of the commercial executive's central responsibilities:

1. How to organize sales teams to sell most effectively

2. What roles to hire

3. How to arrange those roles into teams

4. How to make sales teams work

For a long time, the standard answers to these questions seemed given:

Hire salespeople. Organize salespeople into teams of similar sales individuals. Have them work individually to achieve their individual targets, as the way for the company to achieve its overall sales targets.

The purpose of this book is to give business leaders a new perspective on these questions and how to answer them, in light of the changes that have been taking place in business-to-business buying and selling.

The book is split into five parts that can be read chronologically or in random order, based on the topic most relevant to the reader's specific situation and needs:

1. **Chapter 1:** Why *Teams That Sell* win when selling and buying complexity grows

2. **Chapter 2:** What types of teams are best for different types of sales

3. **Chapter 3:** How to organize sales into *Teams That Sell*

4. **Chapter 4:** How to build and manage *Teams That Sell*

5. **Chapter 5:** How to get started on the transformation

Although the book is for commercial executives responsible for sales organization design, it is also for the people on their sales teams.

It's about leadership's responsibility to make sure that everyone in their organization (including salespeople), have a great place to work, great colleagues to work with, and a company that they are engaged in working for.

BASED ON RESEARCH AND DECADES OF EXPERIENCE BUILDING TEAMS THAT SELL

The contents of this book are backed by extensive research and illustrative real-life cases, written by people who have spent decades building *Teams That Sell* both in their own businesses, and for some of the world's largest business-to-business enterprises.

As business owners, we have built *Teams That Sell* in our own businesses in the professional services industry—most recently at Kvadrant Consulting, where 80% of the staff play different roles in our selling efforts, from opportunity leads and solution architects, to proposal writers and key account managers.

Get a competitive advantage from the way you sell.

As consultants, we have spent the past decades helping some of the largest business-to-business enterprises in the world define and succeed with their most important sales and marketing transformations, aligning and motivating sales leaders, managers, and people around new improved ways of selling and managing sales.

Lastly, as leaders in our own organization and as consultants to others, we have seen what a difference it can make to people's engagement and motivation when we stop obsessing about sales as an individual performance discipline and change the lens to view selling as a team effort.

A paradigm shift from an old regime wherein salespeople were set up and treated as lone wolves toward one wherein different types of people with complementary capabilities work jointly in sales to radically transform sales performance and give the company a competitive advantage from the way they sell.

We hope you enjoy this book.

Martin Nyvang Mariussen

Partner, Kvadrant Consulting

Thomas Børve Jørgensen

Managing Partner, Kvadrant Consulting

Sixten Schultz

Partner, Kvadrant Consulting

"It is the long history of humankind that those who learned to collaborate and improvise most effectively have prevailed."

Charles Darwin

INTRODUCTION

WHY YOUR NEXT SALES HIRE MIGHT LOOK NOTHING LIKE YOUR LAST

In the fall of 2019, we were working with a European production equipment manufacturer, who had come to us with a particular problem we had started to see more and more of over the years.

Their company was unable to hire enough qualified salespeople who met their specific criteria, and the scarcity was creating an inability to meet growing company sales targets.

The company had an offering that was relatively new to the market and was expecting that within the next five years, market penetration of the category was going to move from just 1% in 2019 to 20% in 2024. Whoever was able to capture that growing share would enjoy significant lock-in effects with the customers they were able to acquire.

In other words, the company was in a hurry to grow sales and grow the sales organization.

Over the past six months, the CCO that we were working with at the company had invested significant time and money on internal recruitment efforts and on a headhunting firm to fill the vacant positions.

Despite their efforts, there just weren't enough qualified people coming in to fill the recruitment pipeline, or at any rate the hiring was moving too slowly. Not because there weren't any salespeople to be hired in the countries where they operated, but because they were hunting for a special type of sales specialist.

This specialist had to be a salesperson who, on the one hand, had technical expertise to manage the technical discussions in the sales process (e.g., an electrical engineering degree), and on the other hand, had the ability and desire to sell complex solutions to large customers in different production industries like chemicals, pulp and paper, and manufacturing.

Putting more money behind renewed recruitment efforts was not likely to produce any results fast enough and a new approach to the problem was required.

Throwing additional resources into hiring efforts was not likely to bring about any significant results.

Acknowledging that perhaps throwing additional resources into hiring efforts was not likely to bring about any significant results, we discussed with the CCO whether there was a different way to look at how we might solve the sales resource bottleneck.

Instead of asking how to get more of the same type of salespeople they already had (electrical engineers with enterprise selling expertise), we wondered what would happen if we asked:

> *"How might we get more out of the salespeople that we already have?"*

HAVING EVERYONE DO EVERYTHING IS NOT AN EFFECTIVE WAY OF SELLING

The heart of the problem was the way the company organized selling.

The European sales organization was split into seven markets, with sales teams of 4–6 people in each of these covering different target customer segments. Each individual sales team member was assigned their own smaller geographical area to cover.

These assignments showed a classic divide-and-conquer approach, where each salesperson is given their own account portfolio, covering a specific customer segment and area, and given responsibility for growing sales in that area.

Within their own areas, each salesperson was asked to run a sales process end-to-end on their own:

- **Territory management and resource allocation:** Research market to specify the strategy for time allocation based on assessment of potential

- **Demand generation and prospecting:** Research accounts to identify new potential customers and stakeholders to engage with and establish initial connection to identify and create leads

- **Opportunity creation:** Meet with target stakeholders to create qualified sales opportunities through interest creation and needs discovery

- **Opportunity management:** Create a business case for change and get buying committee buy-in for the changes. Demonstrate the solution and deliver technical proof of value and feasibility for the customer's specific setup. Negotiate and sign the final contract

- **Solution implementation:** Help new customers manage the implementation process of the new solution

- **Account management and development:** Conduct ongoing meetings with key stakeholders in customers' organizations to strengthen relationships and create new opportunities for expanding account values

- **Purchase order handling:** Take care of new purchasing orders from customers and make sure these are processed to deliver additional products and services

In essence, the old paradigm had every single salesperson do everything, from prospecting and closing to account management and order taking.

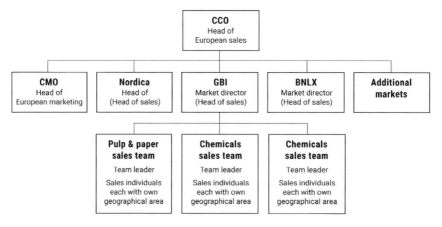

*Figure 1: **Organization Chart.***
Organizing sales into groups of individual sales reps.

In general, this creates the following three major challenges to effective sales work:

1. Time is spent on tasks that might be important, but where the sales professional is not adding a lot of value (and others might have more relevant skills to do better)

2. Time is taken away from tasks where the sales professionals add high value and that only they can do well

3. Time is spent switching between different tasks

Now, those inefficiencies might not be a problem for a company if (a) the unit economics of having the salesperson are still good (i.e., they are contributing the required sales and profit), AND (b) if you can easily find the additional salespeople required to grow sales.

In this specific case, the unit economics of hiring more salespeople were great. There just weren't enough salespeople to invest in.

SCALE WHAT ONLY YOUR SALESPEOPLE CAN DO, AND GET OTHERS TO DO THE REST BETTER

Not knowing the company very well at this point, or the types of customers they were serving, we decided not to challenge whether the activities themselves were right or wrong, but instead to focus on whether it was right, from a sales effectiveness perspective, to have scarce sales specialists do all the work.

We asked the salespeople and managers three questions:

- *How is your time allocated to the different tasks you are responsible for?*

- *What are your sales specialists' unique capabilities, and where do these add the most value?*

- *What do you think someone else might be able to do better than you?*

Across all markets the answers came back, painting a clear picture of what the sales organization thought was the right solution to the company's scaling problems.

- Sales spent 15% of their time identifying new potential customers to target and researching these to find relevant information and contact details, but non of the salespeople thought they were very good at it and 95% thought a specialist focused on that specific task would do it better.

- Sales spent 10% of their time managing lists with leads that had previously indicated interest, but none (0%) thought they added much of value in doing so, and 100% thought someone else could do it more effectively.

- Sales spent 25% of their time in technical discussions with operational stakeholders of the customers they were in a selling process with, aligning on how their solution would technically work in their production, how it would impact their supply-chain operations, and what kind of service requirements would be needed for different types of scenarios. All of the sales reps agreed that it was an important activity that right now only they could do, but 80% of them also thought that someone else, such as technical specialists who focused exclusively on this, would be able to do it just as well (if not better).

These answers meant that if we could get others to do prospecting research, lead management, and operational due diligence instead of the existing salespeople, we would effectively:

1. Have doubled the size of the salesforce, by giving them twice as much time to focus on tasks where their unique knowledge and abilities delivered the highest value.

2. Make the salespeople even more effective by having other types of "specialists" do the remaining things better than the salespeople.

Focus on new roles that could make each sales team greater than the sum of its individual parts.

Knowing from experience where technical sales professionals in these kinds of sales organizations typically added most and least value, we agreed with the salesforce's recommendations about how to better scale their limited sales resources.

The answer to the challenge was not to find a smarter way for hiring more of the same type of salespeople that the team already had at that point.

It was to shift focus away from salespeople as individuals, and instead look at new roles that could make each sales team greater than the sum of its individual parts.

In this case, that meant hiring for two new types of roles on the sales teams that we knew had the potential to do just that, and that were easier to find and recruit to the teams:

- An inside sales rep, to take responsibility for lower complexity commercial tasks that did not require the combination of deep technical and complex selling expertise and could be done without meeting customers face-to-face.

- A technical specialist, to take responsibility for purely technical tasks required during the sales process and ongoing account management interactions with the customer's technical stakeholders

USE TEAMS THAT SELL TO LIFT THE SLOPE OF THE SALES EFFECTIVENESS CURVE

Instead of trying to find and hire sales unicorns with both technical and complex selling expertise, we went looking for two other types of people, who had never worked in sales before:

- Inside sales reps (to be recruited from customer service)

- Technical specialists (to be recruited from after-sales service)

Because of the need for speed in both hiring and onboarding new people to the sales organization, we decided to look internally for new hires that would fit our two hiring criteria:

- Very likely able to do assigned tasks better than the salesperson

- Available to hire in all our markets (or, as a minimum, in the largest ones initially)

What we hypothesized, and later confirmed when the new sales teams went live, was that sales teams that consisted of (1) salespeople with engineering degrees, (2) inside sales reps and (3) technical specialists would outperform sales teams that had only the original salespeople on the team

In other words, implementing *Teams That Sell*, rather than teams of sales individuals, would not only address the company's scaling problems (i.e., free up time for scarce salespeople with sales skills plus engineering backgrounds), but also make the sales team more effective as a whole, by bringing in other types of specialists focused on owning specific sales tasks.

*Figure 2: **New Sales Team Composition.***
Complementary roles to increase sales efficiency and effectiveness.

- One **Inside Sales Rep** to take responsibility for
  - identifying new potential accounts and stakeholders to engage with,
  - establishing initial connections with target accounts and stakeholders to nurture and qualify before handing over to sales, and
  - managing a growing list of qualified leads that need additional nurturing before being ready to start buying process (the right person and company, but not the right time).

- One **Technical Sales Specialist** (an engineer without commercial skills) to take responsibility for
  - solution configuration during the sales process,
  - technical due diligence during the sales process to ensure a fit with customer operations,
  - development of an implementation plan for the later stages of the sales process and the handover to the operational customer management team.

- Three to four **"traditional" Technical Sales Professionals** with responsibility for
  - creating sales opportunities from leads and prospecting targets generated by inside sales,
  - managing active sales opportunities from start-to-finish , but supported by new team colleagues,
  - negotiation and closing, and
  - managing account teams on selected large accounts.

Just three months after the first two *Teams That Sell* went live in the UK pilot market, they had not only demonstrated that this new type of team was able to scale their sales organization (two new types of teams selling as much as two types of traditional teams), but also that they were able to sell more effectively by having different types of specialists collaborate around completing the complex task of selling.

> # The next hire for your sales team might look nothing like the last.

This successful pilot effort is why the next hire for your sales team might look nothing like the last, and why we wrote this book.

THE DECLINE OF PROFESSIONAL FUNCTIONS AS THE DOMINANT ORGANIZING PRINCIPLE

At the heart of the problem (or opportunity) is the growing disconnect between how commercial organizations are traditionally organized and how customers actually buy today.

Although modern buyers use a mix of digital, virtual, and physical channels interchangeably throughout their entire buying process, commercial organizations tend to organize into functions split by the type of customer engagement they specialize in, leading to a siloed and disconnected customer journey.

Marketers in marketing teams take care of digital engagement. Sales development reps in inside sales teams take care of virtual engagement. Field sales reps in sales take care of face-to-face engagement.

Professional expertise is the dominant organizing principle instead of a customer-centered structure.

So far, commercial organizations have turned to joint KPIs, writing formalized partnership agreements or even physically placing the different people closer to each other in the office to bridge the gap between the different functions.

And although organizations with strong sales and marketing collaborations and alignments see 25–30% higher 3-year revenue growth and growth in profitability from higher win-rates, higher customer retention, higher ROMI, and shorter sales cycles[2], such results do beg the question:

> *"If successful selling in the new buying environment requires a team of specialists (e.g., marketers, inside sales reps, sales executives, etc.) to work together to deliver the required buyer journey and experience, why are we organized into separate functions instead of cross-disciplinary teams?"*

AS BUYING GROWS IN COMPLEXITY, THE CURRENT ASSEMBLY LINE APPROACH TO SALES AND MARKETING STOPS MAKING SENSE

The past decades have seen a revolution in innovation and product development, as traditional waterfall approaches have been replaced by agile development.

Instead of designers handing over work to engineers, who hand over work to programmers etc., work is done in cross-disciplinary teams around achievement of a shared objective.

We call it a new paradigm because it transcends the traditional manufacturing view of production (the assembly line), which works best in environments with little uncertainty and low complexity.

For the past century, this "assembly line" approach, where sales and marketing work in sequence (marketing creates demand and leads,

---

2. https://www.kvadrant.dk/2020/06/19/six-ways-btb-marketing-functions-can-make-themselves-indispensable-to-sales/

sales sell and manage accounts), has been the dominant paradigm in business-to-business selling and has shaped the organization into a marketing function with marketers and a sales function with sellers.

But selling in business-to-business is no longer as simple as generating awareness and demand through marketing and then coordinating teams of salespeople to convert demand into sales:

- The buying process has become digital and virtual: Besides meeting physically with vendors, business-to-business buyers now use, on average, six digital channels through the entire buying process and prefer to engage virtually with vendors in 75% of buying situations.

- The buying process has become more complex: business-to-business buying now happens in a buying committee of, on average, seven people with an overload of information to interpret, thus increasing the complexity of decision making.

- The buying process has become messy: 90% of business-to-business buyers report looping back and forth in the decision-making process.

This means the classic handover from marketing to sales does not exist in reality, and with business-to-business buyers using a mix of digital, virtual, and physical channels throughout the entire buying journey, the need for marketing and sales (face-to-face and virtual) to collaborate around the entire buying journey grows.

In this kind of environment, an assembly line approach to organizing the commercial organization does not work, and we need to move towards a new paradigm of collaboration for complex problem solving.

ORGANIZE AROUND CUSTOMERS INSTEAD OF PROFESSIONAL DISCIPLINES

The separation of marketing, inside sales, and sales departments is such a stable part of any business-to-business company, that we forget they are in fact professional disciplines which have just traditionally been split into separate departments to drive the achievement of one thing:

> *Profitable growth in the target customer segments that the company serves.*

And with a growing number of customers adopting a mix of channels when buying, a mix of professional disciplines are required for delivery. That increasingly means that the commercial organization requires teams of people with different areas of professional expertise to sell and deliver the required customer journey and experience.

Instead of separate teams split by professional disciplines, we need cross-disciplinary teams of both sellers and marketers (tech and data specialists, etc.) organized around the customer and the way they buy today.

The future commercial organization is organized by its ability to engage with customers.

As business-to-business buying complexity grows, the need is increasing for teams of sales, marketing, and other specialists, each with their professional expertise, to collaborate around achievement of these primary commercial objectives, rather than focus on their own individual areas of expertise.

The future commercial organization is organized not by its distinct professional disciplines (sales, marketing, data, technology etc.), but by its ability to engage with customers, with cross-disciplinary teams collaborating who put the customer at the center.

THE CASE OF SMART TECHNOLOGIES

In his 2022 HBR article "Traditional B2B Sales and Marketing are Becoming Obsolete,"[3] B2B sales researcher and writer Brent Adamson shares the story of Canadian-based education technology provider SMART Technologies.

Having observed the shifts in how their buyers buy, the company's commercial leadership team had become acutely aware of the growing disconnect between how they were selling and organizing their commercial organization (into functions centered around different professional disciplines), and how their customers were buying (through a mix of channels).

This disconnect resulted not only in missed opportunities to drive engagement and growth with both existing and prospective customers, but also in costly and inefficient duplicative efforts around messaging, analytics, and even technology housed in traditional silos that no longer made logical sense.

Instead of investing resources in putting systems in place for better alignment and collaboration between the different commercial functions, the company took a more drastic approach and dismantled traditional sales, marketing, and customer success functions altogether and reconfigured the 250 people in the commercial organization into what SMART labels "Unified Commercial Engines."

---

3. https://hbr.org/2022/02/traditional-b2b-sales-and-marketing-are-becoming-obsolete

In 18 months, lead volume went up 50%, lead acceptance increased 35%, and most dramatically, year-over-year growth stood at an incredible 48%, all during a global pandemic.

Having transitioned teams of individuals into *Teams That Sell*, they achieved impressive growth by realigning the way the company sells and organizes selling to fit the new business-to-business buying environment.

"Great things in business are never done by one person. They're done by a team of people."

Steve Jobs

CHAPTER 1

TEAMS WIN WHEN COMPLEXITY GROWS

Key takeaway

If the complexity of selling is also growing for your organization, you need to consider whether sales should still be organized into *Teams That Sell* instead of groups of individuals.

Most sales teams are made up of 4–10 salespeople led by a sales manager, who each work individually on driving sales in their own designated areas, through customer acquisition and account development activities.

Although we most often call it "a team," it is, strictly speaking, a working group, although granted the word "sales team" does sound a lot better than "sales working group."

Although most organizations have evolved to call collections of smaller numbers of individuals a "team," there are two very different types at play in most companies:

- **A team** is a small number of people with complementary skills who are committed to a common purpose, set of performance goals, and approach for which they hold themselves mutually accountable (Katzenbach & Smith, HBR 1993)[4]

- **A working group** is a small number of people that come together to share information, perspectives, and insights; to make decisions that help each person do his or her job better; and to reinforce individual performance standards. But the focus is always on individual goals and accountabilities (Katzenbach & Smith, HBR 1993)

Teams are very different from working groups when it comes to goals, ways of working, capabilities, and accountability.

The two types of groups share similar characteristics by being collections of small numbers of people, but are very different when it comes to goals, ways of working, capabilities, and accountability.

---

4. The Discipline of Teams (hbr.org)

	TEAMS	WORKING GROUPS
Definition	A small number of people with complementary skills who are committed to a common purpose, set of performance goals, and approach for which they hold themselves mutually accountable.	A small number of people that come together to share information, perspectives, and insights; to make decisions that help each person do his or her job better; and to reinforce individual performance standards. But the focus is always on individual goals and accountabilities.
Goal	Collective	Individual
Ways of working	In synchronization	In parallel
Role capabilities	Complementary	Similar
Collaboration	Through work (operational)	Through knowledge sharing
Synergies	Positive	Neutral
Accountability	Towards other team members	Towards manager
Pros & cons	Effective at higher complexity problem solving, but at expense of efficiency from individual focus and higher coordination cost	Efficient at lower complexity problem solving, but ineffective in solving more complex problems

*Table 1: **Teams vs. Working Groups***

From a commercial leadership perspective, the important distinction to be aware of between "groups" and "teams" is that one is best for solving more simple tasks and the other better at solving complex ones.

- If you have more **simple tasks** to solve, *people working individually alongside each other* (in **groups**) is the more effective way, because little value can be extracted from collaboration and the performance of the group can be maximized by maximizing the performance of the individuals.

- If you have more **complex tasks** to solve, *people working together* (in **teams**) is the more effective way, because high value can be extracted from bringing different capabilities together and individual performance is highly dependent on that of other team members.

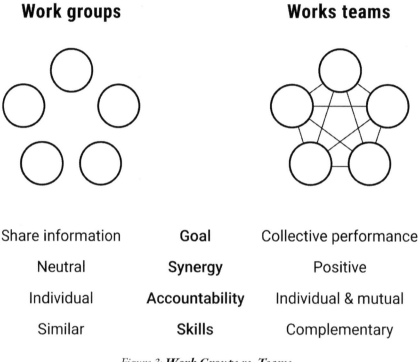

Work groups		**Works teams**
Share information	**Goal**	Collective performance
Neutral	**Synergy**	Positive
Individual	**Accountability**	Individual & mutual
Similar	**Skills**	Complementary

*Figure 3: **Work Groups vs. Teams.***
Difference between two different types of groups with people.

This may seem like academic semantics, but for sales leaders it is an important distinction to understand, because although selling may not be as complex a task as sending a rocket to the moon, it has become a lot more complex than it used to be, and this changes how they might need to approach structuring their sales organization into teams.

THE TYPE OF SALES TEAMS STRUCTURE YOU NEED DEPENDS ON THE COMPLEXITY OF WHAT YOU SELL AND SOPHISTICATION OF HOW YOU SELL

Regardless of whether your company is selling industrial machinery, professional services, or software, sales is ultimately about two things:

- **The customer buying journey:** How to start more of them, win more of them, increase the value of them, and run them with fewer required resources.

- **The customer development journey:** How to keep more customers buying, how to grow their lifetime value and how to make them advocates and ambassadors.

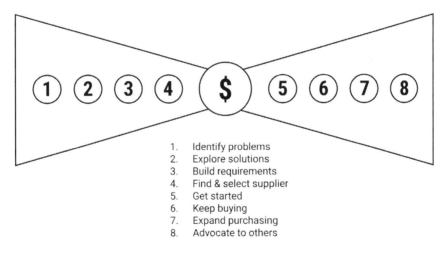

1. Identify problems
2. Explore solutions
3. Build requirements
4. Find & select supplier
5. Get started
6. Keep buying
7. Expand purchasing
8. Advocate to others

*Figure 4: **The Butterfly Sales Development Funnel.***
Buyer and customer development journey.

How much you sell, and the profitability of those sales, is a direct function of sales and marketing's ability to initiate, win, and extract value from customer buying and development journeys.

Although the lines between sales and marketing are blurring, it is, roughly speaking, the salespeople's responsibility to activate and drive customer buying and development processes through direct people engagement (calls, in person meetings, personal e-mails, virtual meetings etc.) while the marketing organization is responsible for doing so through indirect engagement (LinkedIn campaigns, website banners, Superbowl ads, sales enabling material, etc.).

It is the leader's responsibility to decide how to best organize people around the customer buying and development journeys.

It is the leader's responsibility to decide how to best organize people around the customer buying and development journeys, with the following three basic setups to choose from: islands, factories, and teams.

- **Island setups**—each individual sales rep is given broad responsibility for growing sales to their own narrow customer segment, and sales teams are just collections of salespeople, each working on their targets.

- **Factory setups**—people with the same specialization are grouped together into functional expertise teams, such as inside sales, field sales or customer success, working sequentially along the customer buying and development journey.

- **Team setups**—people with different specializations (e.g., marketing managers, inside sales reps, sales professionals, and customer success managers) are combined into teams that work together around the shared overall objective of growing revenue from the team's target customer segment.

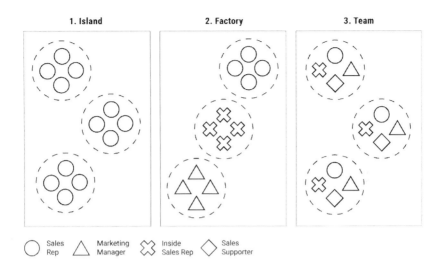

Figure 5: ***Three Types of Sales Organisation Setups.***
Island, factory, and team.

It is important to note that one setup for a sales team organization is not superior to the others in absolute terms.

Although there are fewer and fewer sales organizations for whom an island approach is the best solution, as effective selling grows in complexity, the sales leader's choice of setup for sales depends on understanding the characteristics of each, their pros and cons, and what kinds of sales organizations and situations each is best suited for.

	ISLANDS	FACTORIES	TEAMS
Description	Work groups with broad responsibilities for individual members, along the entire sales process Sales teams as a group of generalist sales reps, with end-to-end responsibility within their designated area or customer segment	Work groups with narrow responsibilities for individual members, for specific parts of the sales process Sales teams as a group of specialists with narrow responsibility, covering a specific part of the sales process (prospecting group, lead mgmt. group)	Sales teams as a group of people with complementary capabilities, collaborating most effectively to grow sales in a designated area or customer segment, for the team
Strategy	Divide-and-conquer	Maximize efficiency	Maximize effectiveness
Types of team members	Generalist sales reps	Specialized sales reps	Complementary specialists
Performance	The sum of individual performance	The product of inter-team team performance	The product of intra-team performance
Target	Individual	Individual & team	Team
Specialization	None	Between teams	Within teams
Good fit for	Low complexity sales with broad product portfolio (e.g., selling cleaning supplies to offices)	Medium complexity sales with narrow product portfolio (e.g. selling simple SaaS solutions or insurance sales)	High complexity sales with customized solutions (e.g., hospital IT systems or industrial bio-solutions)
Pros	Easy to set up and easy to manage	Efficient in stable environments	Effective at complex problem solving and agile around changes
Cons	Ineffective as complexity grows	Does not react well to changes	Higher coordination cost within team

*Table 2: **Islands, Factories, and Teams.***
Characteristics of the three types of sales organisation setups.

1. ISLAND SETUP

Working groups of individual salespeople that are identical, working parallel to each other on their own designated geographical areas or customer segments.

The island setup is essentially a *divide and conquer* approach to selling, in which a market is split into smaller parts that can be covered by different sales teams and those parts then split again into sizes manageable by individual salespeople.

The individual salespeople have responsibility for conducting whatever activities they deem necessary to generate sales from the customer segment allocated to them, and when each salesperson achieves their individual sales targets, the team achieves its overall targets.

> The great thing about the island setup is how easy it is to setup and manage.

Seen from a leadership perspective, the great thing about the island setup is how easy it is to setup and manage. After salespeople are hired who all have similar skills and characteristics, they are grouped under sales managers that get the *teams* to succeed by getting each *individual* to succeed. There is little need to spend time on collaboration, and the performance of one team member is not dependent on how others are doing.

The island setup remains the most common in traditional business-to-business companies for the following three reasons in particular:

BENEFITS OF ISLAND SETUP

Allocation of responsibilities	It is easy to allocate clear responsibility and accountability, when an addressable market is split into smaller parts to be managed by individual people who each get a target.
Easy to identify drivers of poor team performance	It can be isolated to individual team members not reaching their performance targets.
Easy replacements	It is easy to change a member of the team for a new one, with no dependence on other team members.

While island setups are becoming increasingly rare as the preferred organizing principle for sales teams, in a buying and selling environment that is growing in complexity, it is still an excellent solution for companies with certain characteristics:

- Small companies with low sales maturity

- Low complexity sales of broad product portfolios

- High need for geographical customer proximity

The big problem with island setups is that they become increasingly inefficient and ineffective as the sales organizations they are deployed in grow in sales maturity and sophistication.

CHALLENGES OF ISLAND SETUP

Salespeople inferior to technology at simple buying tasks	As transactional order takers, they are inferior to their companies' new e-commerce and self-service channels for making simpler and repeated purchases.
Salespeople have too low level of expertise for high complexity tasks	As sales professionals, they fall short of buyers´ growing requirements for domain expertise and ability to use new channels of engagement in larger buying committees.

In a world where buyers demand speed and simplicity for transactional purchases and expert advice and guidance for complex ones, it is difficult for the average sales generalist to compete.

It means that many companies often start with an island team structure, but as they grow and mature, they move on to new and more effective ways of organizing selling roles and responsibilities.

2. FACTORY SETUP

Sales teams are split into functional specialist teams and arranged along a *factory line*, where one specialist team precedes the next.

For example, the sales team might contain an inside sales team consisting only of sales development reps that hunt for new leads and manage incoming leads from marketing, a sales executive team consisting of salespeople that guide new buyers through the purchasing process and close deals, and a customer success team consisting only of customer success managers that manage customer orders and grow business engagement with existing accounts.

This represents a conveyer belt of specialist teams (or working groups, to be absolutely correct) comprised of individuals with the same capabilities, roles, and responsibilities, converting market potential into new customers, and creating growth in existing ones.

> Factory setup focuses on operational excellence.

The factory setup is a more advanced divide and conquer approach to selling than the island setup, where different parts of the customer journey are allocated to different specialist teams, each responsible for their individual parts.

Each specialist team is given a performance target that relates to their designated area of responsibility in the commercial engine, like an inside sales team measured on their ability to generate qualified leads and pipeline value for sales, a field sales team measured on their ability to close new sales and a customer success team measured on their ability to retain and grow existing customers. What is unique about the factory setup is how the performance of each specialist team is highly dependent on how well other teams perform, because of how they are connected.

On each specialist team, individuals have similar skills and characteristics and work on achieving their own individual performance target with little collaboration between team members. Sales management focuses on operational excellence within the teams and ensuring dependencies between teams are managed continuously.

The factory setup for sales teams is perhaps most known from its wide use in high growth Software-as-a-Service (SaaS) sales, where a scalable setup with high operational efficiency is critical.

Its use, however, is not limited to SaaS. Instead, it is widely used by companies across a broad range of business-to-business industries, especially those that have a narrower product portfolio or fewer types of target customer segments and work in relatively stable business environments, for three reasons in particular:

BENEFITS OF FACTORY SETUP

High operational efficiency	Each team specializes in repeatedly performing a narrow subset of tasks to perfection.
Simple to scale	Each team can be expanded or duplicated based on needs to grow the business.
Predictable outcome and business metrics in stable environments	The performance of the machine can easily be modelled and efficiency measured in its respective parts.

Operational efficiency does however not come for free. The factory setup has the following three major drawbacks that make it less than ideal for many sales organizations:

CHALLENGES OF FACTORY SETUP

Unagile in adapting to process input variation and task changes:	Each cogwheel is set up to perform a set of pre-defined tasks to perfection, based on assumptions about quantity of work to be processed (number of leads to qualify, sales qualified leads to hand over, deals to close etc. per week, month, quarter, year) and the customer types and opportunity types to be managed (which needs to be narrow, to allow for standardization of work). If business fluctuates and selling is too complex to put into a standard cookie cutter approach, a factory setup will create problems.
If one team does not perform, the entire commercial engine does not perform:	In factory setups, each team's performance is dependent on the performance of other teams. If there´s a business development rep (BDR) team responsible for prospecting for new leads and a sales development rep (SDR) team responsible for qualifying and converting those leads into SQLs, both will fail to deliver business value if just one of them breaks down. If the BDR team does not perform, the SDR team does not have enough input to process. If the SDR team does not perform, the BDR team´s work becomes wasted.
Potential for a messy customer experience:	In factory setups, customer stakeholders are passed from team to team, as they progress through their buying and customer development journey, which increases the risk of a choppy buying journey with added friction. An example would be a lead passed on to sales, but not followed up on for days.

It means that for companies managing one or very few types of buyer–customer journeys (because they have few target customer types and a narrow product portfolio), with a need to scale fast with operational efficiency, factory setups can be great (as shown by their wide adoption in

SaaS companies that basically sell one solution with variations of it based on customers adoption) to few types of target audiences.

But for most traditional business-to-business enterprises in industrial manufacturing, MedTech, IT enterprise solutions etc., that is not the case—these businesses require a setup better equipped to manage the complexity of selling in these industries.

3. TEAMS THAT SELL

Teams That Sell combine different specialist roles on the same sales team to collaborate around growing sales to their target customer segments.

For example, a MedTech company might have a sales team targeting the hospital customer segment, consisting of inside sales reps (to generate new leads and sales opportunities, and manage customer purchase orders), account executives (to manage and develop business relationships, and engagement with hospital business decision-makers), and technical specialists (doctors or nurses to activate and nurture medical staff who use the products on a daily basis).

Teams That Sell are capable of combining different specialist roles around a shared goal of growing sales, with each person taking care of different aspects of selling that they are experts in, so that each specialist maximizes time spent on what they do best.

Although each specialist role on the team still has their specific KPIs related to the aspect of selling that they are responsible for, success is ultimately measured by how well the whole team performs. This means that although collaboration and knowledge sharing are high within the team, there is little collaboration among teams, because each team has the capabilities required to complete the entire selling process on their own.

From a leadership perspective, the big difference between island and factory setups and *Teams That Sell* is how team leaders in the first two setups are mainly focused on managing individuals. Leaders of *Teams That Sell* are primarily focused on making the team work as a whole.

The team sales setup is perhaps best known for its wide use in sales organizations with high needs for technical capabilities in combination with commercial capabilities—for example, MedTech companies that combine salespeople and medical professionals like doctors or nurses, industrial bio-solution companies that combine salespeople with chemical engineers, or enterprise software companies with both salespeople and IT specialists.

People with complementary skills work together to succeed better than they could have individually.

Like a soccer team with different specialist roles (goalkeeper, defenders, midfielders, strikers), rather than a group of strikers all trying to score.

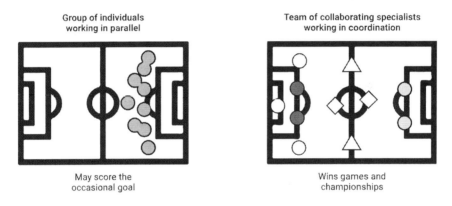

*Figure 6: **Working in Parallel or Working in Coordination.***

Creating sales teams that are actual teams with complementary skills working together, rather than working groups, is growing in popularity as selling in business-to-business becomes more complex, for the following four reasons:

BENEFITS OF TEAMS

Teams are more effective at complex problem solving	If you want to make cheap clothes you use island or factory setup, but if you want to send a rocket to Mars, you use teams of people with complementary capabilities.
Teams make for more effective distribution of labor	Roles on teams that require higher monetary compensation can maximize the time they spend on what only they can do (for example, a doctor in a MedTech company sales team) while other team members that might merit lower monetary compensation can focus on what they do best (an inside sales rep performs tasks that they can do better than the doctor).
Teams are more agile around changes	If circumstances change in the team's selling environment, the team has a broader range of capabilities and resources to adjust to these changes.
Teams drive higher employee engagement	People that work on teams are more engaged in their work than people whose work is primarily carried out while working alone.

However, despite the potential benefits of working in *Teams That Sell*, and their better fit with a selling and buying environment that is growing in complexity, it would be wrong to believe that this is the miracle cure to solve every sales organization's problems. First, it is not the right setup for all sales organizations.

Those organizations with selling characteristics that better match an island or factory line setup might find that sales effectiveness declines by implementing a true sales team structure, because the increased cost of collaboration or loss of focus by only managing a narrow set of repetitive tasks.

And just like the island and factory setups, *Teams That Sell* comes with its own set of challenges:

CHALLENGES FOR TEAMS THAT SELL

Higher coordination costs	The team´s success is dependent on frequent and ongoing communication that aligns each member around the shared tasks and objectives at hand.
Higher transformational requirements	For sales organizations that have been accustomed to a sales setup with a high focus on individual performance (individual responsibilities, individual performance goals, individual bonuses etc.), moving towards playing as a team is a difficult transformation. It requires not only a change in how people are organized and work, but in the sales culture embedded in the organization, from an individual performance focus to a team performance focus (more on this in chapter 5).
Different sales management requirements	Whereas sales managers in island and factory setups mainly have to be skilled at 1–1 people management and managing people who are *similar* in their skills and responsibilities, managers of *Teams That Sell* have to build, develop, and manage a team of people who have *different* skills and responsibilities. Like the goalkeeper trainer who has been promoted to head coach of the soccer team, it is a change that comes with responsibilities and new capability requirements.

For the commercial leader it means that moving to a *Teams That Sell* approach is no free lunch, although it might be the right move to make.

It requires not only well-thought-out changes of roles, responsibilities, and ways of working, and also an upgrade of sales management capabilities, an update of sales culture, and investment in the success of the transformation.

Because commercial leadership must constantly weigh the potential benefits of transformation for tomorrow against the potential risks of disturbing the ongoing business of today, it is beneficial to look at salesforce transformation as an evolution rather than a revolution.

Look at salesforce transformation as an evolution rather than a revolution.

Although the right end destination might be *Teams That Sell*, the right thing to start with might be a factory setup with an inside sales team—a traditional sales team and a customer success team working sequentially—and then evolve further from this new platform of sales organization maturity.

In this way, the development of how to organize around selling is a lot like the evolution of how car manufacturers have organized around making cars.

The automotive production process has evolved from being done by *islands* of individual craftsmen, to being produced on conveyer belts with great efficiency, and finally to being made by teams to manage the growing complexity of car manufacturing.

Just like the complexity of effective car manufacturing has grown because of changes in the internal company environment (e.g., more complex products) and the external environment (e.g., changes in buyer preferences), the same is happening in sales.

WHY TEAMS BECAME KEY TO MODERN CAR MAKING

If you are in business, you have heard the story before. But like all great stories, it does not grow old from being retold.

The year was 1908, and the place was Detroit Michigan. Henry Ford and the Ford Motor Company had been working for a few years on making a car that would realize the founder's vision of "motor cars for the great multitude,"[5] with releases of models A, C, F, N, and ultimately the now infamous Model T.

But Ford had a big problem.

To realize his vision of a car for the masses, he needed to find a way to greatly increase the efficiency of the car-building process to lower production cost, so that the cars could be sold at a price point suitable for the masses.

Enter the Ford factory assembly line. The complex process of car building broken down into 84 discrete steps, where you could train and assign individual workers to master just one of those steps.

Reducing the time to build a car from 12 hours to 1 hour and 33 minutes and succeeding in putting a price tag on the car that even his own workers could afford to buy.

Ford model-T sales went from 17,000 in 1913 when the whistles on the assembly line floors were first blown, to 2,000,000 units just a decade later.

The story of Ford and the assembly line is in essence the story of the great industrialization, Adam Smith, and pin making: production moving from small islands of individual artisans and craftsmen towards scientifically managed factory floors of individuals working in sequence, to reap the efficiency gains that came with it.

From individuals that do everything themselves, toward individuals coordinated to work in sequence as a group.

The idea was to manage complex production by industrializing it, in everything from pottery and steelmaking to cars and electrical appliances.

That is how it worked, until it didn't work anymore.

---

5. https://college.cengage.com/history/primary_sources/us/henry_ford_discusses.htm

FROM FACTORIES OF INDIVIDUALS TO AGILE TEAMS

Meanwhile in 1918, halfway across the world, another company was founded that just like the Ford Motor Company was to become the stuff of business legends.

Toyota.

Originally a loom production factory (and in fact it still is[6]), Toyota's company management had travelled to the US in the late 1920s, to investigate automobile manufacturing and by 1936 had launched its first passenger car, the Model AA.[7]

The company was a slow starter, having reached just 2% of the US market share 40 years later—meanwhile, General Motors accounted for a whopping 40%[8] in the 1970s

But then something happened.

From 1980 to 2006, Toyota's share of the US car market more than quadrupled, from 3% to 13%, and has continued to rise to 15% today (2020),[9] although the car manufacturer's road to success was not always a linear one, it was an upwards moving one.

Entire books could be written (and have been) about the reasons for Toyota's success, but among its key factors have been their unique production and supply-chain systems, which include lean, just-in-time, and Kanban.

The great insight for the company was that a Ford Model T factory approach to production worked incredibly well when you have just one car type to produce in just one color (black). Their process could be broken down into 84 discrete sequential steps that could each be managed

---

6. History of Toyota - Wikipedia

7. History of Toyota (toyotauk.com)

8. Lessons from Toyota's Long Drive (hbr.org)

9. Car sales market share by country, manufacturer and quarter - CSIMarket

by an individual worker and could be repeated over and over again until perfection.

The problem appears when complexity rises, as it has done over the years since the introduction of assembly line-produced Fords in 1913.

Growth in model types, car sophistication, and customization options, as well as the globalization of supply chains, had moved car making from a relatively simple process to one that required a different type of production approach.

The ability of multiple people with different roles and responsibilities to collaborate in real time and make adjustments to their activities based on signals from both inside from the factory business, and outside from the market.

Companies with agile operations can react and act fast to changing circumstances.

Although the time required to make a car has not changed much since the introduction of the Ford assembly line, the productivity improvements are remarkable considering the cars that modern manufacturers churn today out versus those of 100 years ago.

At the heart of the car manufacturer today is the Toyota Flow System, "a system of patterns, practices, and techniques to enable organizations and institutions to achieve desired outcomes in a complex world."[10]

Because complexity grew, Toyota put the team at the heart of their business, as one of the core pillars of the manufacturer. This business philosophy was the completely opposite of the Ford Motor Company's philosophy a century earlier.

Although the assembly line was right a century ago, when car making was difficult but simpler (84 steps to making a car), it became ineffective as a way of working in the new environment. The inefficiency helped a new operating philosophy come to light.

---

10. The (Toyota) Flow System | On Lean and Agility (lean-agility.de)

*Figure 7: **The Toyota Flow System**.*

In complex environments, teams that work together, rather than collectives of coordinated individuals, get the job done.

However, even though car production went through radical transformation throughout the 20th century, the selling process remained virtually unchanged.

Right until everything changed.

Selling has never been easy, but it used to be simpler.

AS COMPLEXITY GROWS SO DOES THE NEED FOR TRUE TEAMS IN SALES

Another area of business under rapid transformation, more familiar to us than automobile supply chain and production, is business-to-business selling.

But unlike the car industry, which gradually changed from its invention in the late 19th century to the present, sales remained virtually unchanged up until the beginning of the 2000s.

Salespeople would prospect through calls or participation in industry trade shows and conferences. Sales meetings would be done in person. Contracts were closed face-to-face or via fax and mail. Account management happened over steak and red wine.

While selling might once have been done by one person through meetings with relatively few people who had limited access to information, this is no longer the case. Instead, research clearly shows that this has radically changed over the past decades.

Selling has never been easy, but it used to be simpler, and the drivers of higher complexity for salespeople working in business-to-business sales come from both external sources (from changes in the buying environment) and internal sources (from changes in the company).

They will have more people to sell to and a messier sales process to manage. This will mean less time, with more opinionated buyers who involve sales later in their buying process and more channels to manage for customer engagement.

It is not only developments in the external buying environment that salespeople work with that are changing and making successful selling more complex. The companies they work for and the sales organizations they work in are on the move too.

KEY DEVELOPMENTS IN THE EXTERNAL COMPANY ENVIRONMENT

More people involved in the average purchase:

Between 2015 and 2017 alone, the number of people involved in the average business-to-business buying process grew 26% from 5.4 to 6.8.[11]

The development toward having more stakeholders involved makes successful selling more challenging with the purchase likelihood getting stuck growing with the size of the buying committee,[12] with 15% of their time now spent on "deconflicting information."[13]

It makes selling more complex, because more roles with different perspectives need to agree on shared problem to fix, align on a buying vision, and select a solution that all feel meets their needs the best.

If the sales department does not do a good job, the risk is that the buying committee gets stuck and moves on or that the only thing they can agree on is that it needs to be the cheapest.

Buyers looping back and forth in the buying process

90% of buyers now report "looping back and forth" in their decision-making process.[14]

The development toward a messier, nonlinear sales process makes successful selling more challenging because salespeople constantly have to realign their selling activities to what the customer is now focused on in their buying journey.

It makes selling more complex—for sales to do the right things at the right time, they must constantly understand what the buyers are focused on and move forward from there.

Less time with more informed buyers

From 1994 to 2014, the share of buyers that get their information primarily through their own information gathering more than doubled,[15] with sales reps now only getting 5% of the buyer's time during their purchasing process[16] and buyers having already gone through most of their buying process before reaching out to vendor salespeople.[17]

This makes selling especially challenging for salespeople with less of a chance to shape their understanding of their customer's pains and needs in the beginning of their buying journey.

They will have less time with the buyer to gain that understanding and create the compelling reasons for buying

	their offering.
Changing buyer preferences for how to engage	Buyers now use an average of 6 channels to find information during their buying process,[18] and in 75% of buying situations, they prefer to meet with vendors through remote engagement[19] rather than face to face.
	For salespeople this means that to successfully engage with buyers where they are and where they want to engage, they need to learn how to master new channels for customer engagement and be able to decide when to use which channels for different types of customer interactions.

11. The New B2B Sales Imperative (hbr.org)

12. The Power of People – Donal Daly / 6 Rockets

13. https://www.gartner.com/smarterwithgartner/what-sales-should-know-about-b2b-buyers-in-2019/

14. How B2B Sales Reps Use Customer Interactions to Close Deals (gartner.com)

15. Demand Gen Content Preferences Survey 2018 - what B2B buyers want from vendors, James Barclay (passle.net)

16. The New B2B Buying Process | Gartner

17. Study: Half of B2B Buyers Make Up Their Minds Before Talking to Sales Reps | Miller Heiman Group

18. Make Content Experiences the Epicenter of B2B Customer Engagement (mrpfd.com)

19. Are You Listening? Many Customers Prefer Inside Sales (salesbenchmarkindex.com)

KEY DEVELOPMENTS IN THE INTERNAL COMPANY ENVIRONMENT

Growing product complexity	Most physical products are becoming increasingly complex and have often both data generators and processors on top of their mechanical properties.
	Also, the boundaries between software, hardware, and services are blurring.
	For this reason, new business, delivery, and payment models are constantly emerging.
Higher frequency product launches	The pace of innovation is increasing with not only new company offerings coming out more frequently, but also updates and changes to existing offerings, as companies move toward products with software built in for on-going updates.
	For sales, this means additional work in staying on top of the company's product and service portfolio and investing time in understanding its value proposition and how to communicate with customers about it.
Growing dependency on collaboration with marketing	Sales and marketing organizations that rate their collaboration as strong have 24% higher average annual growth rates and 27% higher profitability than average[20].
Greater use of new technology	The number of sales and marketing technology applications has gone from a few hundred in 2011 to thousands of digital tools today,[21] with a median of 9 tools being used in the average sales organization.[22]
Growing amount of data and information	Companies' data on customers is no longer limited to what sales had time to put into the CRM system, but comes from a growing number of digital channels, such as e-commerce portals, loyalty programs, digital behaviors on websites, engagement with digital marketing campaigns or the customers' own digital footprints.

---

20. https://www.superoffice.com/blog/sales-marketing-alignment/

21. Marketing Technology Landscape Supergraphic (2020): Martech 5000 -- really 8,000, but who's counting? - Chief Marketing Technologist (chiefmartec.com)

22. 6 sales tech stats from the latest SST report that may blow your mind (membrain.com)

Salespeople have more complex products to sell and new ones to sell more often. They have a greater need to collaborate with marketing and new requirements to make use of a growing number of sales enabling technologies and data to use for decision-making.

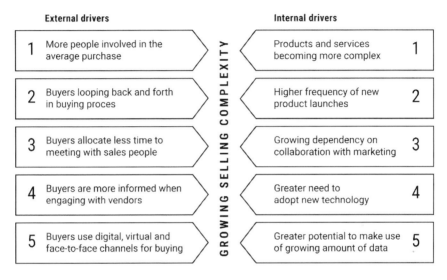

Figure 8: **Drivers of Growing Sales Complexity.**
External (market) drivers and internal (company) drivers.

As the external selling environment has grown more complex with evolving and maturing buyers, so has the internal environment in which sales operates with evolving and maturing companies.

This means that most sales teams should be set up as real teams of people with complementary skills working together, but in fact they are not.

Despite selling growing in complexity, working groups with individuals that have the same skills doing the same thing in parallel remains the dominant way of organizing sales teams.

While other parts of business organizations have responded to growing complexity by shifting from working groups (e.g., most product development teams, which are now comprised of people like programmers, designers, UX specialists, engineers, and marketees), the majority of sales organizations have chosen a different path.

Attempt to make each sales individual **absorb growing complexity at an individual level** rather than as a team.

CONTINUING TO ASK SALES INDIVIDUALS TO DO MORE IS NOT A SUSTAINABLE WAY FORWARD

Until a decade ago, the different types of roles on the average business-to-business marketing team could be counted on one or two hands, including a few generalists focused on the different areas of marketing responsibility (area, brand, and product) and specialists focused on creative output (copy, design, and production). The team roles included the following:

- Area marketing manager

- Brand manager

- Product marketing manager

- Copy writer

- Designer and creative producer

These roles reflected what marketing was responsible for at the time and the complexity of the activities they were engaged in.

But as business-to-business buying behavior changed and marketing organizations started adopting new channels, tools, and technologies to improve effectiveness and efficiency, the roles of the marketing organization also changed.

One website[23] now boasts a collection of 75 digital marketing titles alone, that have popped up over the past decade. These new titles include Social

---

23. https://www.drift.com/blog/digital-marketing-job-titles/

Media Managers, Paid Search Managers, SEO Specialists, Marketing Automation Specialists, Data Analysts, Ninjas and Rockstars.

SEO Specialists, Marketing Automation Specialists, Data Analysts, Ninjas and Rockstars.

The dominant logic behind the growth of specialist roles in marketing has been that of meeting increased maturity and associated complexity in operations with specialization rather than broadening each individual marketing manager's responsibilities.

Rather than asking existing marketing managers to become broader generalists, the marketing organizations brought on new specialist roles to the team and became more effective through collaboration.

Although marketing organizations matured and managed new tasks and responsibilities through onboarding new specialist roles to the team, many sales organizations went down a different path.

That path meant asking each individual salesperson to do more.

What we know from sales research over the past decade is that these developments have greatly influenced what is required to be successful in business-to-business sales, particularly in the following five ways:

FIVE REQUIREMENTS FOR SUCCESSFUL B2B SALES

1. Navigate complexity	Successful salespeople have a sales process as their backbone,[24] but are able to use their own judgement to navigate a messy buying process, instead of blindly following a pre-defined sales process, to perform better (although the majority of salespeople are still more "process compliant-orientated").[25]
2. Challenge and prescribe	Salespeople are able to challenge[26] the customer on their existing way of thinking, to change their already "informed" minds and be proactive and prescriptive in their recommendations about what they believe is right for the buyer and the right way to move forward in their decision-making process,[27] to help them deconflict tension and uncertainty in the buying committee.
3. Embrace new channels of customer engagement	Successful salespeople are able to engage with customers not only through face-to-face meetings, but also through social media, virtual meetings, and other new channels where buyers increasingly spend their time and have a preference for engaging with vendors.
4. Embrace technology	Top salespeople are more likely to embrace technology,[28] and describe themselves as "power-users" of their company's sales technology and company-wide technology platforms.[29]
5. Guided by data	Salespeople are 2.7 times more likely to be "top-performing" when using granular data to guide decision-making on what to do with specific customers or opportunities and have a "playmaker" that helps use data to suggest sales plays for different sales situations[30] (hint: a new sales team member that grows sales and sales effectiveness).

24. https://hbr.org/2015/01/what-top-sales-teams-have-in-common-in-5-charts

25. https://hbr.org/2013/11/dismantling-the-sales-machine

26. https://www.gartner.com/smarterwithgartner/power-challenger-sales-model

27. https://hbr.org/2017/03/the-new-sales-imperative

28. https://techseen.com/sales-report-linkedin-2017/

29. https://www.linkedin.com/pulse/what-separates-strongest-salespeople-from-weakest-steve-w-martin-1c/

30. https://hbr.org/2021/08/the-sales-playbook-of-successful-b2b-teams

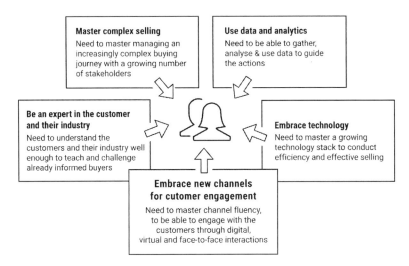

Figure 9: **Growing Sales Professionel Requirements.**
Many roles to master to succeed as a B2B Sales Professional.

In other words, the salesperson you want needs to have deep selling expertise, customer expertise, guts to challenge informed buyers, channel fluency, tech savviness, and data analytics skills.

In addition to HR's problem of finding—and hiring—these sales super-stars or trying to develop the existing people in the salesforce into them, continually piling more demands onto salespeople has had another unfortunate consequence.

Technology—supposed to be the great savior of salespeople´s time—has eluded most salespeople.

One 2022 study from Salesforce.com (2022 State of Sales Report) found that only 28% of salespeople's time was spent on selling activities with customers and 72% was spent on other tasks (such as administrative tasks, CRM, research) and that technology, which is supposed to be the great potential savior of salespeople's time, has eluded most salespeople and for some even added more time-consuming responsibilities to their to-do list.

As sales organizations continue to develop and mature with the purpose of taking advantage of new changes in their buying environment and new possibilities for how to sell, they keep adding new requirements for what their existing sales individuals need to do and be able to do:

- Be a **thought leader**, creating content to be used especially on social media channels

- Be a **mini-marketer**, engaging in social selling on social media channels

- Be a **data analyst**, using the internet and databases to gather information and analyze it for decision-making

- Be a **bionic sales rep**, mastering a growing sales tech stack of sales enablement and customer engagement tools

- Be an **inside sales rep**, using virtual and digital channels for customer engagement with buyers who increasingly prefer remote interactions

- Be a **challenger**, who understands the customer's industry and business well enough to teach them something they don't even know

- At the same time, be an efficient **transactional sale rep**, that can accommodate customer purchasing order requests

It is not that any of the new requirements are wrong. The most effective sales organizations do engage in thought leadership, social selling, data analytics, hybrid selling, use of various technological tools, etc.

The problem is that continuing to pile responsibilities on the individual sales rep level comes with three major risks:

INDIVIDUAL SALES REP OVERLOAD RISKS

Sales effectiveness goes down	If the core capability of salespeople is to engage directly with existing and potential customers to drive profitable sales of a company's offerings, then sales leaders risk taking away focus from what they do best (engagement) when they broaden their list of responsibilities and instead have them spending time on what they are not great at (e.g. writing thought leadership content or searching and analyzing data). Taken all together, these shifts lower sales effectiveness instead of increasing it.
Employee engagement goes down	In his 2011 book *Drive*,[31] author Daniel Pink identifies three things that drive employee engagement and motivation: *Purpose* (people see meaning in their work), *autonomy* (people are given freedom to make decisions), and *mastery* (people spend their time doing what they want to master). The latter (mastery), for most salespeople, is about excelling at helping specific target audiences identify new ways to improve their businesses and helping them through a buying process to realize the potential value of their company's offerings. When sales leaders ask salespeople to perform tasks outside their field of mastery, they risk lowering employee engagement.
Top-line can't grow	Good salespeople are hard to come by and for industries that have technical requirements (medical, engineering, IT etc.), even harder. For organizations where that is the case, growth may be held back by the inability to find enough qualified sales professionals. Here there is a need to find ways to scale those technical salespeople in scarce supply, to have them spend more time on what only they can do, and less time on what others might be able to do better.

---

31. Drive: The Surprising Truth About What Motivates Us: Pink, Daniel H.: 8601420442870: Amazon.com: Books

As it doesn't look like development will stop any day soon, or even slow down, continuing to ask salespeople to do more is likely not a sustainable path for sales leaders to follow.

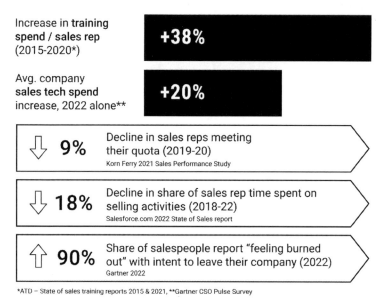

Increase in **training spend / sales rep** (2015-2020*)

+38%

Avg. company **sales tech spend** increase, 2022 alone**

+20%

⬇ **9%** Decline in sales reps meeting their quota (2019-20)
Korn Ferry 2021 Sales Performance Study

⬇ **18%** Decline in share of sales rep time spent on selling activities (2018-22)
Salesforce.com 2022 State of Sales report

⬆ **90%** Share of salespeople report "feeling burned out" with intent to leave their company (2022)
Gartner 2022

*ATD – State of sales training reports 2015 & 2021, **Gartner CSO Pulse Survey

Figure 10: ***The State of B2B Salespeople.***
Investing more than ever but salespeople not better off.

To avoid stretching the work of each individual salesperson to the point where effectiveness, engagement, and growth decline, the work needs to be done at the team level rather than at the individual level.

But this shift in how to approach selling is no easy feat to navigate, because it changes the fundamental way that we have looked at selling since its beginning and continue to look at it today.

We look at selling as an individual discipline won at an individual level. **To change sales, we have to fundamentally change the way we look at selling.**

TO LIFT SALES WE HAVE TO FUNDAMENTALLY CHANGE THE WAY WE LOOK AT SELLING

There are many good reasons why it makes sense for sales leaders to shift their sales teams from work groups towards (true) teams:

- True teams are a more effective way of solving the task of selling, as company and customer developments make it a more complex one to solve, requiring people with complementary roles, responsibilities, and capabilities to come together.

- True teams reduce employee turnover rates in the sales organization, increase employee satisfaction, and make people more effective at their work, because people who work on teams are more engaged in their work than those who work individually.

- Ture teams reduce the risk of the *inability to hire qualified salespeople*, becoming a bottleneck to growth, because working as a team can free up time for more customer engagement by those people specifically hired for that role on the team.

- True teams make people on each team responsible for effective customer engagement (i.e., salespeople), more effective at the core high value aspects of their job, because there are other people on the team to cover the aspects where they are less skilled (e.g., gathering and analyzing data).

- True teams improve profitability from lowered cost-of-sales, because not all people on the sales team needs to be highly paid customer engagement salespeople, and because working on teams leads to higher job satisfaction that can reduce people's need for monetary compensation.

As selling grows in complexity, shifting to *Teams That Sell* has the potential to accelerate growth, increase employee satisfaction and engagement, reduce risk, increase overall sales effectiveness, and improve profitability.

This of course begs the question:

Why haven't most sales leaders already moved from teams of individual sellers towards Teams That Sell?

At the heart of the problem is how we have been trained to look at sales and selling since the birth of the professional discipline:

As an individual one.

Individual sales territories, individual targets, training on how to be a better salesperson at an individual level—all aspects are considered through an individual lens.

Although the journey might be right, as highlighted by examples from the introduction and potential benefits listed above, it is not an easy one.

The shift from organizing sales into teams of individuals towards *Teams That Sell* requires fundamental changes to not only the composition of roles on sales teams, but to the entire system around sales in terms of salesforce design, hiring, management, compensation, development and culture.

It requires first **revisiting the fundamental blueprint** for how sales is organized.

The shift from organizing
sales into teams of
individuals towards Teams
That Sell requires first
revisiting the fundamental
blueprint for how sales is
organized.

KEY TAKEAWAYS

- There are three fundamental ways to structure sales teams: Islands, factories or true team setups.

- Island setups are good for low complexity sales and are easy to manage. Factory setups are good for high efficiency in sales organizations with a narrow product and segment focus, operating in a stable selling environment. *Teams That Sell* setups are good for more effective selling in more complex selling and buying environments (which is often the result of sales organizations maturing the way they sell and becoming more sophisticated)

- The development in sales is like the industrial development of the 20th century, from the first artisan production of cars, to factory setups when making cars was still lower in complexity, to a team setup today as the complexity of car manufacturing grew.

- Business-to-business selling and buying has grown in complexity over the past decades because of changes in both the external environment (more informed buyers, greater use of many channels to engage with vendors, and larger buying committees) and internal developments in the company and sales organization (more frequent product launches, more complex suite of offerings, and greater use of data and technology).

- As complexity grows, a team approach to problem solving becomes more effective than the traditional divide and conquer island approach, requiring that sales leaders fundamentally change the organization of their sales teams, from teams of sellers to *Teams That Sell*, as they mature their sales organizations and grow with the complexity of selling.

KEY QUESTIONS FOR COMMERCIAL LEADERSHIP

1. **What kind of sales team setup do you have today and what is the rationale for this type?**
   Do you use an island, factory, or team setup to organize selling? What were the reasons that you chose one setup over the others? Does this rationale still hold true, given how your sales organization and its selling environment have changed since it was set up?

2. **How are your internal and external selling environments changing and what does that mean for the way you should be selling?**
   How is the external (market, customer, and competitor) environment changing and how does it influence the requirements for how you should be selling? How is the internal (company and technology) environment changing and how does it influence the requirements for how you should be selling?

3. **What will make your selling efforts successful under the new requirements for the way you sell?**
   Based on new requirements, what fundamental beliefs do you have about what will make your sales teams successful? Customer expertise over geographical proximity? Team performance over individual performance? Sales management as a sales enabler over ad-hoc problem solver?

4. **What would be your business rationale for shifting to *Teams That Sell*?**
   Reduce cost of selling by being able to differentiate pay for different tasks to be done? Grow sales effectiveness by making sure people maximize time on what they can do best? Scale the salesforce, by giving more time for activities that only people who are hard to recruit can do? Improve employee engagement and reduce turnover rates, to make the commercial organization a better place to work?

"None of us are as smart as all of us."

Ken Blanchard

CHAPTER 2

FIVE TYPES OF TEAMS THAT SELL IN B2B SELLING

Key takeaway

The way you need to sell and the type of *Teams That Sell* that you need depends on the type of selling you need to succeed, with roughly five types to choose from, each with their own set of complementary specialists to best grow sales, efficiency, and effectiveness.

It is, roughly speaking, the sales organization's job to activate the customer buying processes, help them through their decision process towards purchase, and help them continuously grow the value they get out of the offerings they buy and the business relationship between them.

The better they do this, the more sales opportunities they create, and the more likely they are to win them and the higher account value their customers have.

Selling is helping customers create value for their business through the right purchase and adoption of products, services, and, broadly speaking, we know well the general characteristics of selling organizations that best succeed with this:

- **They educate and challenge** their customer stakeholders to help them understand new opportunities for value creation in their businesses and learn how to realize these by changing the existing way of doing things.

- **They prioritize time** with existing and potential customers who are actually interested in having their business challenges addressed and where the vendor's offering is a good fit for their specific problems, needs, and situation.

- **They enable decision making** by helping customer stakeholders make sense of abundant information and guide buying committee members through the different decisions they need to make together to buy the best solution for their needs.

- **They ease purchasing decisions** by helping customer stakeholders quantify the potential business cases for addressing a challenge or opportunity through purchase of a product, service, or solution.

- **They build trust** by acting as an advisor to their customer stakeholders and putting the customer at the center rather than themselves.

- **They tailor communication** by asking questions, sharing insights, and making proposals that are tailored to the specific stakeholder, their company, industry, and situation, rather than a generic off-the-shelf script.

- **They remove buying friction** by enabling the customer to conduct buying tasks that they prefer to do themselves without face-to-face vendor meetings, such as placing a purchasing order through self-service solutions or meeting through virtual channels.

- **They maximize time spent on customer engagement and make the most out of this time** by structuring work, taking advantage of enabling technology, and being disciplined around meeting management.

These characteristics create the right activity level, with the right customers, at the right time, done in the right way.

But, as any experienced commercial leader will know, although there are general principles for how to sell most effectively and efficiently, different types of companies set up selling very differently to best help their target customers create value through purchasing.

If the commercial leaders of marketing automation platform Hubspot and aviation engineering company GE Aerospace had to agree on a shared way of selling, similar types of salespeople to hire, and the same sales technology stack to work with, neither would likely do very well.

The reason is that different types of companies and commercial organizations are set up to succeed with different kinds of purchases, which can be roughly categorized into five different types:

Different types of companies need to be set up to succeed with different kinds of purchases.

FIVE TYPES OF PURCHASES

Technical purchases	Purchases that are complex to make because of their technical characteristics, where the value of the purchase is delivered predominantly through product performance.
	These are purchases such as biofuel producers buying new enzymes to add to the production process, making it more efficient and producing higher quality output. Or a contractor buying a HVAC system for a new building project that can make the building operate with lower energy requirements and environmental impact.

	These are complex purchases because they are technically complex, with the buying committee dominated by technical stakeholders.
Enterprise purchases	Purchases that are complex to make because of the broad business consensus that needs to happen to reach a purchasing decision because the value of the purchase is delivered through organizational change rather than product performance.
	These are purchases such as a shipping company buying a new CRM solution to make the commercial organization more efficient and effective and improve the customer experience. Or a professional service company buying a new time registration and invoicing system for better capacity utilization.
	These are complex purchases because of both the solution complexity and the broad consensus required in the business to make a purchasing decision.
Transactional purchases	Purchases that are lower in complexity to make because the products or services being bought are simpler, more familiar to the buyer, and have fewer people involved in the purchase.
	These are purchases such as a professional service company buying cleaning of their offices or a restaurant chain buying napkins and cutlery.
	Simple well-known products or services being bought, where the value of the purchase comes from the performance of the products or services bought.
Functional purchases	Purchases that are lower in complexity to make because the offering is simple and the decision to buy can be made by a small buying committee, but where the value of the offering needs to be realized through adoption of the product or service and change in how people in the business work.
	These are very often purchases of specific SaaS solutions by different functions in the business, such as a marketing department buying access to Canva or an HR department buying access to Contractbook (a contract management solution).
Partner purchases	Purchases that go through a partner or distributor, where selling to an end-customer is done by or with people in the partner organization, who predominantly manage the customer engagement and ongoing relationship.

It matters that commercial leaders are able to distinguish between different types of purchases because they differ with regards to the two things they need to make sure their sales and marketing operating model and capabilities are aligned to

- How customers buy, and

- The buying experience they value when making a purchase.

Whereas technical purchases happen through a longer complex buying process with emphasis on vendors' ability to demonstrate technical proof of value and feasibility, functional purchases happen through a much shorter and less complex buying process with emphasis on vendors' ability to demonstrate the potential business value of solutions if they are adopted by the organization and their ease implementation.

TECHNICAL	ENTERPRISE	TRANSAC-TIONAL	FUNCTIONAL
Who leads buying			
Technical stakeholders	Business stakeholders	Operational stakeholders and purchasing	Functional stakeholders (e.g., marketing or finance)
Key buying and selling journey activities			
Understand new technical advances and potential benefits	Understand new business trends, challenges, and opportunities to address	Understand whether there has been a change in need since the last time a similar purchase was made	Understand and define need and scope for solution
Calculate business case for using product in operations	Define change required in business to address and need to do so	Align with (the few) other stakeholders regarding budget	Decide on budget based on expected time saving and value of offering
Demonstrate technical proof of value and feasibility	Demonstrate potential business value and plan to realize value	Review pricing and products at different vendors	Demonstrate how solution solves the function's needs
Implement technical solution into			Drive adoption of solution with users

operations	Drive adoption of solution in business and adaption to ways of working to realize value	Share offer and practical information with buyer	that need it and adaption to ways of working to realize value
Buying experience drivers			
Vendor technical expertise, ability to demonstrate solution value and feasibility, and help implement into operations	Vendor business expertise, ability to demonstrate business case for change, and help get solution adopted by organization to realize value	Vendor product knowledge expertise, ability to demonstrate benefits, and ease of purchasing and doing business with vendor	Vendor functional expertise, ability to demonstrate simplicity of product use and benefits of doing so and vendor's ability to drive solution adoption in their business to realize value
Key commercial capabilities required by vendor			
Educational content marketing Technical sales reps with business acumen Technical specialists to demonstrate value and feasibility	Thought leadership content marketing Consultative sales reps with domain expertise Product specialists to ensure product and technical fit with buyer's operational and technical stakeholders	Performance marketing (SEO, SEM, Online ads) E-commerce for customer self-service EDI solution for automated purchasing Sales reps with product and domain expertise	Content marketing & lead generation/management Lead qualification & nurturing Consultative opportunity management with narrow stakeholder group Customer success to drive adoption of solution in business

*Table 3: **The Four Types of Direct B2B Buying.***

For commercial leaders to decide which type of purchase—and customer relationship—they need to set up their operating model and which capabilities they need to support, there are two factors that above all influence their decision:

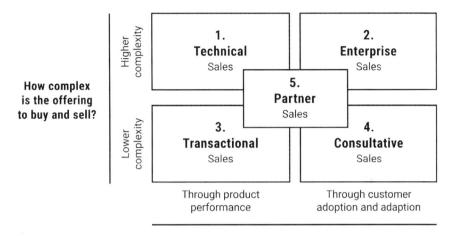

*Figure 11: **Sales Model Decision Matrix.***
What type of selling should the commercial organisation be set up to succeed with?

- **How complex and important does the customer think the purchase of the offering being sold is?** Simple offerings that are easy to understand and low risk to buy (e.g., the company catering service) or more complex offerings that are more difficult to buy with higher associated risk (e.g., the company ERP system).

- **How does the offering deliver value to the customer?** Offerings where the value is delivered by the product itself (e.g., enzymes used in a production process that give higher quality output) or offerings where the value is delivered by how it enables the organization to work more effectively and efficiently (e.g., the company CRM system).

These are the two questions to ask and answer when deciding on the optimal way to set up and operate sales because the answers to these questions determine which capabilities a commercial organization needs to grow sales most effectively and efficiently.

- Sales of **higher complexity** solutions and value delivered through product performance (such as enzyme manufacturers selling to bioenergy companies), requires strong capabilities in educational content marketing, technical expertise, complex sales process management, and key account management.

- Sales of **higher complexity** offerings and value delivered through customer adoption and adaption (such as SaaS companies selling enterprise ERP or CRM systems to large organizations) requires strong capabilities in account-based marketing, sales enablement, solution selling, and key account management.

- Sales of **lower complexity** offerings where the value of the product is delivered through product performance (like building material suppliers selling to dealers) require strong commercial capabilities in e-commerce, performance marketing, sales territory management, and time-management.

- Sales of **lower complexity** offerings and value delivered through customer adoption and adaption (like SaaS companies selling to users in the business) require strong capabilities in lead generation and conversion, marketing automation, inside sales, customer acquisition, and customer success.

In short, the complexity of buying and selling the offering and how the offering delivers value to the customer influence how the commercial organization should be set up to operate and the capabilities that are needed to do so successfully.

What is important for the commercial leader to note is that one company can easily have multiple sales models in operations because of the complexity of their business, what they are offering, and the types of end customers they serve. This can require them to have different types of sales teams and capabilities to operate sales effectively and efficiently.

Take the example of global logistics provider Maersk, which offer everything from complex end-to-end logistics solutions to spot-buy freight:

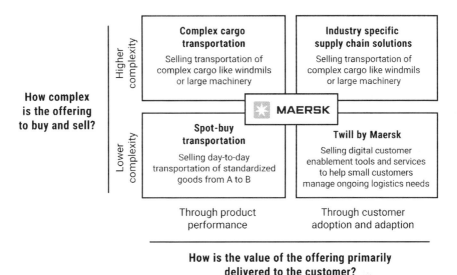

Figure 12: Maersk—Sales Model Decision Matrix.
Example of application to integrated logistics provider Maersk.

- **Technical sales in logistics:** Selling one-off transportation services for high complexity (very large) cargo (e.g., windmills or large machinery) requires a high degree of technical knowledge during the sales process, but little in terms of requiring change in the customer's organization to deliver the value of the service.

- **Enterprise sales in logistics:** Selling end-to-end logistics solutions tailored to fit the specific needs of different industries (e.g., pharma or fashion) where the business value of the solution is extracted through changes in the business, like reducing warehouse stock or being able to keep lower inventory in point of sales stores.

- **Transactional sales:** Selling available capacity on ships, trains, or trucks that are leaving from one destination to another to companies that may need to have some goods transported on the same route at that time.

- **Consultative sales:** Selling new digital tools for use by specific stakeholders in supply chain and logistics companies.

The distinction between different types of sales for different types of offerings being sold to different types of end customers is important to commercial leaders because it guides their decision on what sales operating model(s) to set up to drive sales and growth most effectively in their company and on what capabilities to build in their commercial organization.

All sales models have in common that they have people hired in sales to engage directly with customers.

The commercial leader in a company with an offering and sales type characterized as *transactional sales* would double down on building strong capabilities in digital customer self-service, e-commerce, performance marketing, and inside sales. By contrast, the commercial leader of a company with offering and sales types characterized as *enterprise sales*, would invest in implementing strong capabilities in thought leadership, account-based marketing, sales enablement, and key account management.

Although the sales models are different regarding the commercial activities and capabilities needed, all sales models have in common that they have people hired in sales to engage directly with existing and potential target customers to help with different types of purchases and the development of their business.

The kinds of salespeople they hire; however, does vary, because different kinds of salespeople are needed for different kinds of selling.

DIFFERENT KINDS OF SALESPEOPLE FOR DIFFERENT KINDS OF SELLING

Different kinds of sales organizations hire different kinds of salespeople because selling their offerings to their target audience varies with regards to sales rep requirements to function in their specific commercial operating model and the types of purchases and customer relationships they need to manage.

Selling highly technical solutions to sophisticated buyers (e.g., enzymes to food producers, or electrical power systems to industrial manufacturers) often requires hiring engineers that can sell, while lower complexity products or services to less sophisticated buyers (e.g., cleaning services to offices, or phone subscriptions to small businesses) requires salespeople that can sell.

Depending on what a company sells, how it is sold, and how customers get value from it, different kinds of sales organizations hire different kinds of salespeople.

DIFFERENT KINDS OF SALESPEOPLE

Technical salespeople

These are sales reps with deep technical and functional expertise who are hired for selling that requires (a) deep technical expertise in the solution being sold, and (b) thorough understanding of the solution's application in the customer's business operations.

These sales reps often have higher education within a specific technical area that their company works within, such as chemical engineers working in sales for an enzymes manufacturer or supply chain expert working for a specialized logistics company. They are hired for their technical expertise and credibility and then trained to succeed in a sales role toward sophisticated buyers with similar technical knowledge.

Enterprise salespeople

These are sales reps with deep expertise in selling and in target customers' businesses who are hired for selling that requires (a) a strong ability to activate and manage complex buying processes and customers' organizations, and (b) a strong ability to communicate the business impact of the solutions they sell.

These sales reps often have higher education within businesses specialized in their target customer's type of business, such as hospitality or healthcare. They are hired for their selling expertise towards selected target customer types and then trained for technical and product expertise required for the solutions of the company they sell for.

Transactional salespeople

These are sales reps with expertise in customer engagement, relationship management, and time management to get new customers buying their offerings and grow the contract values over time. They are hired for their ability to create, manage, and develop customer relationships through a high-volume of interactions with a clear objective, with buyers and accounts where the time invested is assessed to most likely lead to growth in sales.

These are the traditional "travelling sales reps" who often come from backgrounds similar to the professions of the customers they are responsible for selling to, but typically without any higher education like that of the technical or enterprise sales professionals. They are hired for their attitude and ability to connect to the buyers they are responsible for selling to, and trained in the offering they sell and the best way to get it to market.

Consultative salespeople	These are sales reps with expertise in buyer engagement to drive forward buying processes with a narrow segment of account and stakeholder types for a narrow solution portfolio. They are hired for their ability to manage a sequence of interactions with their narrow target customer and stakeholder segment to explore potential value, demonstrate solutions, and help their customer get started. These sales reps are the typical SaaS account executives—hired for their intelligence, passion, and adaptability and then trained to drive sales by applying these skills to the specific customer, stakeholder, and product type they are working with.
Partner salespeople	These are sales reps with expertise in driving sales with external parties through relationship development, business development, and partner sales and marketing enablement. They are hired not for their ability to sell directly themselves, but rather their ability to incentivize, motivate, and enable others to do it. Although partner sales reps are also responsible for partner portfolio management, they are hired for having the strong account management and business development skills required to expand business engagement with individual partners in their portfolio.

DIFFERENT KINDS OF SELLING

Selling type	Typical titles	Sales rep characteristics	Example
Technical sales	Sales Engineer	Deep technical and functional expertise and credentials, hired for selling that requires (a) deep technical expertise in solution being sold, and (b) application in customer's business operations.	Electrical engineer in Vattenfall Network Solution
Enterprise sales	Account Executive	Deep expertise in selling and target customers' businesses, hired for selling that requires (a) strong ability to activate and manage complex buying processes and customers' organizations with (b) strong ability to communicate business impact of the solutions they sell	Account executive in Salesforce.com
Transactional sales	Sales Representative	Expertise in sales-focused customer engagement, account management and time-management, hired for their ability to connect with target buyers and manage customer engagement and trained for selling their company's specific offering	Sales rep in Kekkilä, selling substrates for greenhouse food production
Consultative sales	Account Executive	Expertise in customer engagement management hired for their intelligence, passion and adaptability and trained to be able to apply it to the specific target customers, stakeholders, and offering type, they are selling to help them buy and adopt their solution	Account executive targeting small accounts in Hubspot
Partner sales	Partner Portfolio Manager	Expertise in driving sales through others rather than selling directly themselves, with partners that need to be incentivized, motivated, and enabled to drive sales. Hired for their strong account management and business development skills	Export manager at veterinarian equipment manufacturer Kruuse

Essentially sales leaders recruit different types of salespeople with regard to experience, expertise, and capability because of (a) the priorities for what they need the most to sell effectively varies for different types of sales, and (b) what they are willing or required to pay for different types of expertise.

In other words, companies that sell highly technical but high value solutions to their target customers have both a need and a willingness to pay for highly skilled experts to sell, while companies that sell more simple, lower value products to less sophisticated buyers have a lower need and willingness to pay for technical, sales, or customer expertise but instead value the ability to communicate, manage time and activities, and work proactively with customers.

When hiring people for their salesforce, sales leaders make a conscious prioritization of what they believe is needed the most for selling their company's offering to their selected target customers and what they are willing or required to pay for this, prioritizing between different requirements for expertise, capability, attitude, experience, and network.

The challenge is that getting the right people hired in sales to deliver all these traits is rarely possible nor desirable from a business perspective because of the higher cost of these superstar sales reps.

So, sales leaders must prioritize what kind of people they want in their sales organization to succeed with the kind of customers they target and the selling they conduct.

And just like the type of sales*person* a company needs depends on the kind of customers it serves and the type of selling it conducts, so does the kind of sales *team* the company needs, although a sales team consisting of different complementary roles has the advantage of disbursing all desirable traits not in one person, but throughout the team.

OVERVIEW OF SALES SKILLS

Expertise	Customer expertise	Customers experience sales reps who have knowledge and understanding to demonstrate expertise in their industry, type of business, and their specific business.
	Product expertise	Customers experience sales reps who have knowledge and understanding about the products, services, and solutions they sell and how these create value.
	Technical expertise	Customers experience sales reps who have knowledge and understanding about the application of products, services, and solutions in customer company operations.
Capability & attitude	Sales capability	Customers experience sales reps who have the ability to help them start the right buying processes, guide them through it and reduce risk of making poor decisions by addressing what happens after purchase.
	Value extraction capability	Customers experience sales reps who have the ability to help them get formal buying processes initiated and moved forward with a buying committee of multiple people with varying roles and interests.
	Communication capability	Customers experience sales reps who are able to clearly communicate and speak their language when having a discussion of the product or solution in question.
	Proactivity & responsiveness	Sales reps proactively address potential issues to mitigate them and are always responsive both internally and externally toward customers.
	Time & activity management	Sales reps are able to take control of their own time and activities, to work as efficiently as possible at all times, to ensure maximum output of their work.
Experience & network	Ability to get up to speed fast	Sales reps are able to work independently, with limited support, and get to performance fast, because they have done before what they are asked to do now.
	Network in place that fits target buyers	Sales reps are able to activate their own network to take offerings to market. Members of their network would otherwise have been difficult to get in touch with and get time with.

THE TECHNICAL SALES TEAM

Not all sales organizations hire salespeople to take responsibility for selling. For those companies selling into higher complexity purchases where buying committees are dominated by technical stakeholders, the more common approach is to hire technical experts, like engineers, for their ability to engage in a technical dialogue about how the offering being sold will be able to deliver value in the customer's business operations.

Such companies include the engineering or technically heavy companies like Novozymes, who rely on chemical engineers when selling enzymes to biofuel producers, or FLSmidth, who rely on mechanical engineers when selling processing equipment for mining operations.

Although selling in these kinds of companies follows an overall similar process as other high complexity sales, what is unique is commercial leadership willingness to hire salespeople with technical expertise and credentials over strong business selling expertise. They follow this hiring plan for the following four reasons:

- Because customer value comes from product performance for these types of purchases, technical salespeople need the ability to explain new customer opportunities for value creation in technical terms understood by the technically dominated buying committee and in financial terms for the business.

- It is difficult for nontechnical people to manage discussions with technical stakeholders in the customer's organization These stakeholders have a strong say in whether a purchase will be made and what it will be.

- When it comes to making technical improvements to the way their company operates, technical buying committee stakeholders prefer to take their advice from someone like themselves and with the credentials to prove it.

- Demonstrating that the solution being purchased works and is able to deliver performance as discussed in customer's operations is of high importance during the customer's buying process.

For these reasons, these types of organizations hire technical experts, such as engineers, as salespeople who have the technical expertise and credentials to engage with technically dominated buying committees and customers and to take responsibility for selling.

Although technical sales professionals are hired for their ability to conduct customer activities that require a combination of technical and selling expertise, the activities they actually spend time on can be roughly divided into four different types:

Salespeople who have the technical expertise and credentials to engage with technically dominated buying committees.

TECHNICAL SELLING—ACTIVITIES

Those that require both technical and selling expertise:	They engage with technical decision-makers to educate them on new developments and the potential value if used in their company's operations. They guide the buying committee through their decision process of buying a new technical solution. Conducting ongoing interactions with relevant customer stakeholders for development of the customer relationship and business engagement.
Those that require only technical expertise:	They assess the customer's potential for improvement through implementation of new technical solutions into operations and demonstrate the technical feasibility of the solutions in the customer's operations. They develop a post-purchase solution implementation plan and solve ad-hoc challenges related to the solution purchased for the customer's operations.
Those that require only selling expertise:	They prepare meeting agendas, sales meeting material, and sales proposals. They write sales meeting follow-up e-mails and manage customer purchasing orders. They sell smaller products or services to the customer after purchase, such as equipment consumables or service contracts.
Those that require neither selling nor technical expertise:	They conduct market and customer research to identify new selling opportunities. They update data in CRM and manage customer contracts.

For leaders of sales organizations with the characteristics of technical sales, the challenge is that while they would ideally like their technical sales professionals to maximize the time they spend on the activities that only they can do, they can't because they are occupied with all the other activity types as well.

Too little time is left for what only they can do, because too much time is spent on what others could do, and perhaps do better, resulting in the following four consequences:

TECHNICAL SELLING MODEL—RISKS

High cost of sales

Technical experts able to sell complex solutions are as expensive as they are difficult to find, with sales leaders often paying much more for these sales engineers than they would for normal salespeople and definitely more than for people who would be able to take care of tasks *related* to technical sales that do not requiring technical capabilities.

Lack of sales growth because of hiring difficulties

It is never easy to find good salespeople and finding the ones that possess the combination of deep technical expertise and sales capabilities required to succeed with technical selling is even harder. There are not that many engineers that also love selling. For sales leaders, this can create both short-term problems when a person leaves and it takes too long to find a replacement, and long-term problems if they can't hire enough salespeople required to deliver on the company's growth ambitions.

Sales best-practice gap holding back sales

Technical sales engineers are hired to drive sales; generate demand; and create, develop, and close sales opportunities. They also develop customer relationships and levels of business engagement. Although sales are what they are hired for, conducting selling activities to best practice standards is typically also what they struggle with the most, because they are still more interested in solving technical problems than in selling. For leaders in technical sales organizations, this gap to sales best practice is accepted, because they need to have engineers who are hired to sell, but it also comes at the cost of missed sales and growth.

Missing or misaligned marketing

Even for technical sales professionals, marketing is an important driver of successful selling, because technical buyers also use digital channels during their buying and customer journeys. But just as normal sales professionals struggle to make good use of marketing assets, pick up leads generated by them, and align their selling activities with those of marketing, technical sales professionals struggle with this, arguably even more than the average salesperson.

For these sales leaders, moving from teams of individual sales professionals with technical and commercial expertise toward *Teams That Sell* revolves around one key question:

> *How do I get more value out of the scarce—and expensive—resource of my technical sales reps by (a) freeing up their time from low-value-adding tasks they do today, and (b) enabling them to do their high value adding tasks more effectively?*

COMPLEMENTARY ROLES TO INCREASE EFFICIENCY AND EFFECTIVENESS OF THE TECHNICAL SALES TEAM

Although technical sales professionals are required to conduct technical sales, using only people in these roles to drive sales comes with certain trade-offs for the sales leader.

TECHNICAL SELLING MODEL—CHALLENGES

High cost for activities that could be done cheaper	Engineers that sell are expensive because of their unique characteristics of combining technical expertise with sales capabilities. But not all their activities require this combination of expertise and capabilities and could be conducted by other less costly resources.
	Examples of such tasks include handling a purchasing order that comes in from a customer, which is purely commercial in nature, or conducting a technical proof of feasibility and value test, which is purely technical.
	These activities that are purely commercial, purely technical, or neither commercial or technical, could be done by someone else whose salary comes at a lower price point than sales engineers.
Difficult to scale sales that is dependent on hiring scarce technical sales professionals:	Engineers that sell are expensive because their combination of technical and commercial expertise is rare.
	Good salespeople are difficult to find and ones with advanced professional degrees are even more difficult.

For leaders responsible for growing sales through expansion of their salesforce, this can become a real barrier to growth if they are unable to hire sufficient technical sales professionals to support their growth ambitions.

Experts in the technical, but not the most disciplined in sales:

All sales organizations have some slack between their defined best practice for selling and what is common practice in the sales organization. Not all leads are responded to by salespeople within 24 hours. Not all identified prospects get a call or connection through Linkedin. Not all sales meetings get a follow-up e-mail.

For companies that use engineers to sell, this is typically more pronounced than in purely professional sales organizations, because they are engineers first and salespeople second, and rarely the other way around.

For leaders of technical sales professionals this means that while technical expertise might be a prerequisite to sell their offering, having people who aren't the most disciplined professional salespeople is likely also holding back growth.

Makes poor use of marketing to drive sales:

Many sales organizations and salespeople struggle to make good use of their company's investments in marketing and to act as mini-marketers themselves.

Although this tendency is common across all selling types, it is often even more pronounced in technical sales organizations, because of the lower commercial orientation of their salespeople. They engage in lower activity sharing content and insights through Linkedin and are less likely to continuously share marketing content to educate customer stakeholders.

Consequently, the gap between marketing and sales in technical selling is often greater than in the average salesforce, and a greater share of marketing assets go unused.

The purpose of a technical *Teams That Sell* is to help leadership in these types of organizations grow sales faster, and do so more economically, by addressing these challenges with a team of different complementary roles rather than a group of individuals.

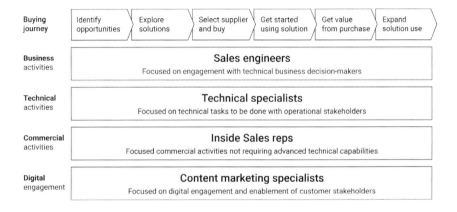

*Figure 13: **The Technical Sales team.***
Four roles to take responsibility for different types of customer activities.

To do so, there are three types of roles for the commercial leader of technical sales organizations to consider as complements to the existing team of technical sales reps or sales engineers, each taking responsibility for different types of activities and engagement with the customer's organization.

TECHNICAL SELLING MODEL—COMPLEMENTARY ROLES

1. Technical specialist

This role has technical expertise and capabilities to conduct purely technical tasks that do not require the ability to sell, to free up more time for the sales engineer to do the customer engagement that drives sales. This specialist assesses the customer's operations to identify potential for improvement through new solutions and sets up technical tests to demonstrate solution feasibility and performance in the customer's operations. They provide support with post-purchase implementation of solution into customer's operations.

The technical specialist is able to take responsibility for all the technical selling activities that go into technical selling at an operational level. They will assess potential, run feasibility tests, and implement solutions with operational stakeholders in the customer organization, so that the technical sales professional is free to focus on engagement with the business decision-makers to create sales opportunities, move them forward, and develop the account. This is a more cost-effective division of labor, because of the ability to differentiate compensation between the two roles. It is a setup that better allows the organization to grow sales, because the technical sales professionals spend more time on the activities that drive sales.

Although the technical specialist shares the same professional background and credentials as the sales engineers on their team, they don't have the same interest or ability to take responsibility for the selling and account management aspects of their job. Hired for their ability to engage with technical stakeholders in the customers' organizations at an operational level, they have the potential to evolve into technical sales professionals over time, building a pipeline of potential future salespeople for the sales organization.

2. Inside sales rep

This person has expertise in lower complexity selling tasks that are purely commercial, can be done remotely, and do not require deep technical expertise and credentials to complete. They free up time for the technical sales professional and make sure that these tasks are actually done and done well. They manage leads that come in from marketing to ensure that the right ones are converted into SQLs to be picked up by the team's technical sales professional. They use customer data and research to prepare material for customer meetings, and handle incoming purchasing orders from customers. They call customer buyers to sell smaller things like equipment, consumables, or service contracts.

The inside sales rep is able to take responsibility for the many different selling and account management tasks where the knowledge and credentials of a technical expert are not required, and which do not require actually going to the customers' sites. The technical sales professionals often have a tendency to down-prioritize many of these activities because they are not where their technical mastery come most into play, but they are nonetheless important for sales. They engage in lead follow-up, purchasing order handling, post-purchase up and cross selling, and are hired for their ability to engage with customer stakeholders through e-mails, calls, and virtual meetings. They are trained to have sufficient technical and customer knowledge to succeed in their interactions.

Unlike their more well-educated technical colleagues, the inside sales reps can come from a range of different educational and professional backgrounds, the most common being business education with remote selling experience from other types of companies and selling.

3. Content marketing specialist

People in this role have expertise in content creation for customers' buying journeys activated through digital channels or salespeople, and take responsibility for indirect customer engagement. They deliver thought leadership presentations to share at events or through webinars, as well as educational content about new opportunities for value creation through use of new technical developments. They share customer reference stories to demonstrate the potential value of solution application to customer businesses and solution buyers' guides on how to assess and evaluate solutions in customer operations.

The marketing specialist on technical *Teams That Sell* can take responsibility for enablement of both customer buying activities and salespeople selling activities via content creation and activation through the right channels. When buying, stakeholders in the buying committee spend 59% more time researching online than meeting with vendors and it is the responsibility of the team's marketing specialist to ensure that the right content is in place on the right channels when they do so.

These people come from marketing backgrounds with a specialty in content marketing, preferably with the ability to manage the added complexity of working in a highly technical business environment. They are hired for their ability to develop an understanding of who their target buyer stakeholders are and how they buy to engage with them through content on the digital channels they use.

Although the technical sales team is still dominated by sales engineers to manage the overall sales process and interactions with key stakeholders in their target accounts, the three complementary roles help the sales leader get the most out of this scarce—and costly—resource, by enabling them to perform high value activities more effectively and free up time from having to perform important but lower-value-adding activities of the technical sales professional.

The three complementary roles of Technical salespeople help the sales leader get the most out of this scarce—and costly—resource.

Take the examples of Novozymes and Ellab, both companies with sales characterized by technical selling and having people with technical backgrounds as salespeople. Novozymes uses technical specialists and Ellab uses inside sales reps to enable their sales engineers.

This structure helps the companies to (1) lower the overall cost of sales by having less costly resources take responsibility for tasks that are either purely technical or purely commercial, (2) make technical sales professionals more effective by having them focus on the critical customer interactions where their combination of technical expertise and commercial capabilities are required, and (3) reduce hiring difficulties by taking pressure off the need for sales professionals with technical backgrounds and, in the case of Novozymes, having a talent pipeline in place with technical specialists that could over time develop into technical sales professionals.

THE ENTERPRISE SALES TEAM

Stating the obvious, all selling requires the ability to help existing—and potential—customers understand opportunities for creating business value through change, gain clarity on what to change to realize this value, and learn how to conduct the change. But for some sales organizations, having people in place that can engage with a diverse group of customer stakeholders to have these conversations matter more than for others.

This is especially true for companies selling higher complexity and business critical solutions, where the value of the offering is primarily unlocked through adoption and adaption by the people in the customer's organization, such as Salesforce.com selling enterprise CRM software or Maersk selling industry specific end-to-end logistics solutions (e.g., ocean transportation, warehousing, and last-mile) to customers in pharma, food production, or chemicals.

Because the vendor's offering is complex and their business critical, with behavior change in the organization required to unlock the value of it, selling in this environment has the characteristics of complex business problem solving and transformation—hence the name enterprise selling.

The enterprise sales process follows similar phases as other high com-plexity sales, from demand generation and opportunity creation, to deal closing and key account development. From research about higher complexity selling,[32] we know the requirements to succeed include the following:

---

32. https://www.amazon.com/Challenger-Sale-Control-Customer-Conversation/dp/1591844355

ENTERPRISE SELLING MODEL—REQUIREMENTS

Taking control of a complex buying process	There is a high emphasis on the sales professional's ability to manage a complex decision-process with a customer buying committee consisting of different stakeholders with varying priorities and interests, from agreeing on the relevant problem or opportunity to address, to agreeing on the solution specification to do so.
Teaching the customer how to address important challenges and opportunities	There is a high emphasis on the sales professional's ability to educate their target customers on new ways to address important challenges and opportunities and how to take advantage of these through changes in their organization and the way they work.
Creating tailored insights and value propositions	There is a high emphasis on the sales professional's understanding of the customer's business and industry, as well as how it operates, so that they clearly communicate the potential strategic and business value of acquiring the solution being sold and the transformation requirements to unlock the value.
Engaging high and mobilizing broad	There is a high emphasis on the sales professional's ability to engage with senior business decision-makers (VP, SVP, CxO) in the customer's organization with high credibility when doing so, and to mobilize stakeholders in and around the buying committee to align and move the decision process forward.
Enabling value realization from a solution purchase	There is a high emphasis on the post-purchase implementation and transformation plan during the sales process, and on the ability of the vendor (or vendor implementation partner) to support the required customer adoption and adaption to gain value from the offering.

Because the primary focus for this type of sale is on how the offering of one business (the selling part) can enable the business operations and strategies of another (the buying part), these types of sales organizations typically hire people with business education and backgrounds in sales and then train them for the specific solution that they are selling. In other words, enterprise sales reps are not necessarily the technical product experts like technical sales professionals, but rather excel at the commercial activities that drive new customer acquisition and growth through existing customers.

ENTERPRISE SALESPEOPLE—ACTIVITIES

Demand generation
Enterprise sales reps continuously inspire key stakeholders in target customer organizations to position relevant challenges, opportunities, and potential solutions that vendor company can help address, through LinkedIn, events, conferences, and meetings.

Prospecting
They connect with target stakeholders in companies not currently customers to create the possibility to generate demand and establish the trust required to enter a formal buying process.

Lead management and opportunity creation
They manage identified leads to convert them into qualified sales opportunities with (a) a buying committee established, (b) a recognized challenge or opportunity to address, and (c) an intent to address a challenge or opportunity.

Opportunity management
They guide the buying committee through their decision-making process, from agreeing on needs and solution requirements to business case, implementation plan, and final purchasing decision. They also mobilize internal stakeholders in their own company who are required to create a proposal and an implementation plan.

Handling purchasing orders
They take care of customer purchasing orders to ensure the vendor organization is activated to deliver the requested products or services and deliver required implementation support.

Account management and business development
They manage ongoing interactions with customer stakeholders to strengthen relationships and expand business engagement.

The enterprise sales professional can establish connections to relevant stakeholders in the organizations of the customers they target, mobilize a complex buying committee to take action and guide them toward a shared purchasing decision in favor of the enterprise sales professional's company. This is high level change management, and no one can do it better than the enterprise sales professional. What sales leaders are paying for when they hire enterprise sales professionals is their customer expertise, sales focus, and strong ability to manage complex customer business decision processes and stakeholder landscapes—from initial contact to purchase, implementation, and ongoing key account management.

For sales leaders dependent on enterprise sales professionals to take their offering to market, there are; however, three big challenges when they dominate a salesforce, not unlike those of the technical sales organization:

ENTERPRISE SELLING MODEL—RISKS

Difficult to find & retain:	Good salespeople are hard to come by, and salespeople with a combination of strong high-complexity selling capabilities coupled with expertise in their target customers' businesses and industries are even harder to find. This scarcity, coupled with the general high turnover rate in sales compared to other business functions, makes getting more value and time out of scarce enterprise sales rep resources a critical task for the sales leader in these types of sales organizations.
High cost of sales reduces profitability:	Highly experienced and capable enterprise sales reps are expensive because they are worth it, bringing in high value deals and growing key accounts. Because of the price tag on these people, the sales leaders who hire them also want to make sure that their time is spent on the activities where the highest return is generated. That typically means more direct engagement with their target customers and less time on CRM data entry or customer data research and analysis, which lower cost resources can easily cover.
Gap between best practice and common practice:	Although it is clear for most sales professionals what they should be doing, a great deal of salespeople in complex sales fall short of this standard due to the high requirements for all the things they should be doing great.

For these sales leaders, moving from teams of individual sales reps toward *Teams That Sell*, revolves around three questions:

1. *How do we use* Teams That Sell *to reduce the cost of selling, by complementing costly enterprise sales professionals with lower cost resources?*

2. *How do we use* Teams That Sell *to help enterprise sales professionals have more time for customer engagement and get more out of that time with the customers?*

3. *How do we use* Teams That Sell *to alleviate hiring challenges and reduce time to performance for new hires?*

COMPLEMENTARY ROLES TO INCREASE THE EFFICIENCY AND EFFECTIVENESS OF THE ENTERPRISE SALES TEAM

We know very well the characteristics we would like enterprise sales reps to demonstrate, such as using data to identify the right topics for different customers' education or using customer verified data and assumptions to tailor the customer business case of a sales opportunity. The problem for many leaders of these types of sales organizations is that the majority of their sales professionals don't actually display best practice behaviors.

Although we know from the research that enterprise sales professionals who educate buyers; tailor messages, value proposition and business cases to fit different customers; and take a structured approach to guiding buying committees through their decision process are the most successful, the same research also estimate that only 27% of sales professionals actually display these behaviors.

Spending too much time on important, but non-customer-facing activities.

The problem is rarely that salespeople don't know what they should be doing to sell most effectively and efficiently, but rather that they are spending too much time on important, but non-customer-facing activities such as opportunity identification or meeting preparation, and they lack specialized the capabilities required to take advantage of new opportunities to get more out of their customer engagement.

ENTERPRISE SELLING MODEL—CHALLENGES

Lack of time for customer engagement	We know from research that although high performing salespeople are able to spend 40–50% of their time on customer engagement activities, average performers spend only 16% of their time on this, primarily because of time spent on (a) opportunity identification and meeting preparation, (b) post-sales customer service, and (c) admin and reporting.[33]
Lack of insights from data on who to spend allocate time to and what to discuss	Sales organizations are 2.7 times more likely to be top-performing when using granular data to guide decision-making regarding specific customers or opportunities,[34] to ensure that customer face time is spent with the right accounts and the focus of the interactions are tailored to fit with the priorities and interests of those stakeholders.
Difficulty of influencing a broad stakeholder group in a buyer company	Although it's true that high performing salespeople in enterprise sales are those that educate stakeholders with tailored content, messaging, and value propositions, this is easier said than done when managing a broad range of business stakeholders in the buying committee, each with different priorities and interests.

To address these challenges there are three roles to consider to complement enterprises sales reps on the sales teams:

---

33. https://www.mckinsey.com/capabilities/growth-marketing-and-sales/our-insights/for-top-sales-force-performance-treat-your-reps-like-customers

34. https://hbr.org/2021/08/the-sales-playbook-of-successful-b2b-teams

ENTERPRISE SELLING MODEL—COMPLEMENTARY ROLES

1. Sales playmaker

With the person in this role has expertise in data gathering, analytics, and preparation of *sales plays* and supporting material for enterprise sales reps, to free up time spent by the enterprise sales reps on opportunity identification and meeting preparation and to help the enterprise sales rep be more effective in their engagement with existing and potential customers by using the most relevant data to prepare material, value propositions, and business case calculations tailored to the customer and stakeholders they are meeting with.

The sales playmaker takes responsibility for the 20% of time an average salesperson spends on using data to identify opportunities[35] and the additional 20% they spend on preparing tailored educational content and messaging in their customer engagement. They monitor data on potential customers to generate insights about good reasons and timing for enterprise sales reps to engage with relevant stakeholders. They also monitor new company hires of relevant roles and recommend messaging and content for the enterprise sales rep to use when connecting. They monitor data on existing customers about their purchasing patterns and changes or news in the company (to generate insights about what to reach out to existing customers about and when to do so) to expand business engagement, and data on how the company is using the solution bought (to recommend potential for up or cross selling to the enterprise sales rep responsible for the account). They gather and analyze company data to create business case calculations for the potential impact of the buying solution.

These playmakers are people with strong analytical backgrounds and the ability to convert data into insights through analysis. They are trained for an understanding of how this is used during the enterprise sales and account management process.

2. Customer success manager

This manager has expertise in helping existing customers adopt the solution they bought and adapt ways of working to maximize the value they get out of buying the solution, to free up time spent by the enterprise sales rep customer engagement at the operational level post-purchase. They also create new opportunities for expanding business engagement addressed by the enterprise sales reps through interactions with customer decisions makers.

The customer success manager can take responsibility for helping customers succeed with the adoption of the solution and the adaption required to maximize the value they get out of it at an operational level, which the average sales professional spends 15% of their time on (versus only 5% for high performers). Having a role on the team to take responsibility for how much value the customer gets out of the solution does; however, go beyond simply freeing up more enterprise sales rep time for customer engagement. The more value the customer gets out of their purchases, the lower the risk of customer churn and the greater the possibility for creating new sales opportunities through greater volume on existing offerings bought, extension into new offerings, or upgrading to more premium offerings.

These managers are people who don't necessarily come from sales backgrounds, but rather customer service professions trained to take a more proactive approach to helping their target customers create value.

3. Account-Based marketing specialist

This specialist has expertise in creating and activating account-based marketing programs for relevant stakeholders in existing and potential customer organizations, to help make enterprise sales rep more effective in their customer engagement activities by having primed and educated stakeholders through other channels than direct engagement with sales.

The account-based marketing specialist can take responsibility for continuously activating a broad range of stakeholders in the sales team's target accounts, with content and communication tailored to fit stakeholders and where the customer is today (potential customer not in the sales process, potential customer in the sales process, or new customer). Although the average business-to-business buyer spends 17% of their time when buying with direct vendor engagement, they spend 27% researching independently online,[36] which is where the account-based marketer comes in to play. This specialist sets up digital marketing programs geared toward nonexistent customers that enterprise sales reps are prospecting on, centered around educating stakeholders on important challenges and opportunities the solution addresses. They set up digital marketing programs geared toward accounts the team is in the sales process with, centered around educating the buying committee on *how* to buy a solution to prime key influencers and decisions makers in the organization. They also set account social selling programs with educational content to be activated through the team's enterprise sales reps' social media channels.

The role of the account-based marketing specialist is to grow the effectiveness of the enterprise sales reps by engaging with target account stakeholders, primarily through digital channels, to reap the benefits of an omni-channel approach to selling.

35. https://www.mckinsey.com/capabilities/growth-marketing-and-sales/our-insights/for-top-sales-force-performance-treat-your-reps-like-customers
36. https://www.gartner.com/en/sales/insights/b2b-buying-journey

Because direct customer engagement is still the primary driver of sales results, the enterprise sales team is typically still dominated by enterprise sales reps, complemented by the three additional roles. Having complementary roles helps the enterprise sales leader maximize the time enterprise sales reps spend on customer facing activities, helping them get more out of those activities and helping them create more opportunities to sell to both potential and existing customers.

> # Having complementary roles helps the enterprise sales leader maximize the time enterprise sales reps spend on customer facing activities.

Take the examples of Simcorp, an investment and data management software provider using both sales executives for new customer acquisition and account development while complimenting them with customer success managers to support value realization of the solution for their customers[37] and presales reps to act as enablers of the sales executives responsible for customer engagement.

This model helps companies like Simcorp (which sells high complexity solutions where value is delivered through adoption and adaption by the buying organization) lower the cost of sales, by having complementary roles that cost less than their sales executives, while enabling their sales executives to have more time for customer engagement and gain more out of those engagements.

---

37. https://www.simcorp.com/en/services/success-management-services

THE TRANSACTIONAL SALES TEAM

Sales organizations characterized by having a transactional sales model, where the complexity of the offering being sold is simpler and the value is in the performance of the offering itself, follow a *land-and-expand* approach, where sales center around creating contracts with new customers and expanding the value, scope, and quantity of purchases over time. The approach includes the following five distinct characteristics:

1. There is high emphasis on the sales professional's ability to identify and address potential demand from existing and current customers (before others do).

2. There is high emphasis on the sales professional's ability to convert incoming customer purchasing requests that come in through e-mail, text, and phone (falling outside the vendor's established customer self-service channels) into sales.

3. There is high emphasis on the sales professional's ability to present and demonstrate product advantages and benefits, especially in terms of differences to offerings from competitors.

4. There is high emphasis on the sales professional's understanding of how their customers buy their products on an ongoing basis and their ability to enable the customer to make the job of buying more easy and effective, as well as less demanding of resources.

5. There is high emphasis on the sales professional's ability to establish, manage, and develop customer relationships that keep buyers from establishing trading relationships with competitors and enables the sales professional to expand their use of their company's portfolio of offerings.

These are the companies that offer broad product or service portfolios to customers that need to buy them on an ongoing basis for use in their business, such as Finnish company Kekkilä, which sells substrates and fertilizer to professional growers of plants and food or Danish company Kruuse, which sells a broad range of equipment for the veterinarian industry.

Historically this was perhaps the most prominent type of salesperson, armed with a product catalogue and classical sales capabilities in relationship management, product pitching, and a high customer engagement activity level.

It's arguably also the type of salesperson that has seen the greatest transformation over the past decades as customer purchasing of lower (and even higher) complexity products has moved to different types of customer self-service platforms (e-commerce) or even been entirely automated (EDI solutions), while buyer preferences for vendor engagement have shifted further toward more remote engagement (virtual meetings).

What has primarily changed for sales reps working in these kinds of companies and sales organizations is the degree to which they need to work with technology to be effective and efficient at the job. This change is regardless of whether it comes to using prospecting efficiency tools and new digital channels for initial engagement or identifying up or cross sell opportunities from customer purchasing patterns and getting the customer to self-service through the company's e-commerce channels.

Transactional sales are interesting, because when we look at the research done on characteristics of high performing salespeople, we see that although salespeople who have the characteristics described in the previous section on the enterprise sales team (teach, tailor, take control, engage high and broad) clearly stand out as high performers, this is not the case for transactional sales.[38] The profile type most likely to be a high performer in transactional sales is the *hard worker*, but without any great distance to other types of salespeople.

---

38. https://www.pipedrive.com/en/blog/challenger-sales-model

Going by the research, what we can however say is something about what high performers in transactional sales are not. People pleasers, focused on getting along with the customer and highly generous with the time they allocate to each of them, finish last in transactional selling.

What the research indicates is that hard work, number of customer interactions and the effectiveness of these matter most in transactional selling, with 3 critical characteristics of high performing reps in these kinds of environment:

1. Maximizing time with buyer stakeholders of target accounts to identify or create new opportunities to sell and convert these to sales.

2. Prioritizing time with buyer stakeholders of target accounts where the probability of getting a return on the time invested, in terms of sales made, is the greatest.

3. Respecting buyer stakeholder's time, has a clear objective for each customer interaction, gets to the point and effectively manages conversation forward with little time to do so.

These strategies point towards the death of the old coffee meeting, which still lives strong in many sales organizations centered around this type of sales but has little merit as a good use of the sales rep's or the buyer's time.

What is more likely, and better in line with our experience working for these types of sales organizations, is that high performing transactional sales teams are those that maximize customer facing time with those accounts most likely to lead to growth in sales. They make the most out of that time by mastering the following five specific areas of responsibility:

TRANSACTIONAL SELLING MODEL—ACTIVITIES

Structured sales approach	They take a structured approach to how they allocate time to potential sales opportunities with existing and potential customers, to maximize return on the time they invest in engagement with buyers.
Customer targeting	They prospect for new potential customers by identifying a good reason to reach out and contacting identified buyers at target companies to create interest that converts into meetings.
Value propostions	They generate demand for new offerings with existing customers by specifying 2–3 great reasons why customers should expand or change what they are already buying and converting the customer to act on this potential through virtual or face-to-face meetings.
Customer relationsships	They manage and develop customer relationships by delivering value in each interaction in the form of "if you do x, you would get y" interactions and not just coming by for a cup of coffee.
Customer satisfaction	They make it easy for buyers to do business with the vendor's company by efficiently converting incoming purchasing requests to orders and helping the customer grow use of the vendor's customer self-service channels.

Unlike the enterprise sales process, characterized by business problem solving and business transformation, transactional sales is about establishing, managing, and developing an ongoing trading relationship with the target customers, which is why companies with this kind of sales model often hire ex-professionals from the kinds of customers they target (ex-gardeners to sell soil and fertilizer to gardeners, ex-veterinarians to equipment of veterinarians, ex-building professionals to sell building materials to current ones) and train them for transactional sales and account management.

Transactional sales is about
establishing, managing,
and developing an ongoing
trading relationship with the
target customers.

Sales leaders hire good transactional sales reps because they need their ability to create, manage, and develop customer relationships through high-volume interactions and clear objectives with buyers and accounts where the time invested most likely will lead to growth in sales.

For sales leaders responsible for transactional sales organizations, there are; however, three major challenges to having a salesforce dominated by individual transactional sales reps, who need to manage a large target account portfolio and a higher number of interactions with clear objectives that convert into additional sales:

TRANSACTIONAL SELLING MODEL—RISKS

A large target account portfolio reduces sales effectiveness

Sales reps working with transactional sales typically have responsibility for hundreds of accounts, covering existing and potential customers, in the segment and area under their responsibility. Analysis of data on the accounts is the right approach to deciding who to invest time in but unfortunately it is often also a very time-consuming approach, when you have hundreds of accounts. As a result, transactional sales reps often allocate time and visits to their accounts based on gut feelings or on who they haven't seen for a while, or simply on customers reaching out to them, rather than based on data driven indications of where the time would yield the highest sales returns.

High interaction frequency reduces sales effectiveness

The number of interactions an average sales rep has with their target accounts varies greatly from selling type to selling type. Because of the higher complexity, enterprise or technical sales teams will have fewer, but higher value, sales meetings than functional sales teams, who have a simpler sales process dominated by remote interactions. For transactional sales teams it is typically somewhere in between, with 3–5 sales meetings per day—still a lot considering that having a clear and meaningful objective for each interaction is a criterion for effective selling. What often happens, when there are 12–20 customer interactions to plan, prepare, conduct, and follow up on per week, is that reps start slacking on how well each of those interactions are prepared and as a result see the returns on those meetings go down in terms of the sales they generate.

The preference for face-to-face interactions hurts sales efficiency

Although there has been a big shift by business-to-business buyers toward a preference for remote interactions with their vendors (and this is now the preferred way to engage with vendors in 70-80% of buying situations[39]), for many salespeople accustomed to getting on the road and visiting customers in person, this is a difficult path to follow. For leaders in transactional sales models, getting sales reps to adopt a hybrid sales approach where they use a mix of digital, virtual, and face-to-face engagement with their target customers, in a way that delivers the best sales return on time invested, continues to be a challenge. The consequence of this overinvestment in face-to-face meetings is lower sales efficiency, because the sales professional is able to do fewer interactions within their available time.

---

39. https://www.kvadrant.dk/2021/01/30/setting-up-virtual-sales-for-long-term-success/

For leaders in sales organizations characterized by transactional selling, the key question to growing sales and sales profitability is:

> *How do I accelerate sales growth by giving my sales reps more time for customer interactions to acquire new customers and to develop business engagement with existing ones, while still enabling them to spend this time with the right customers, about the right things, the right way?*

COMPLEMENTARY ROLES TO INCREASE EFFICIENCY AND EFFECTIVENESS OF THE TRANSACTIONAL SALES TEAM

Transactional sales teams need the following four things to grow sales and profitability:

1. More time for customer facing activities by sales reps,

2. A higher share of those meetings with accounts where time invested results in sales growth,

3. Clear objectives and desired outcomes for each customer meeting, and

4. Well-prepared reasons for each customer to act, shared and discussed in the customer meeting.

Most teams are dominated only by individual sales reps with large account portfolios and busy calendars, which creates three challenges that need the help of complementary roles to grow sales and profitability:

TRANSACTIONAL SELLING MODEL—CHALLENGES

Missing data and analytical capabilities

Although it is common in marketing to use data and analytics to inform ongoing decisions about who to spend marketing budget on and what channels and messaging to use to get the most out of money invested, it is a different story in transactional sales despite having the same dynamics.

Just like marketing investment in spend on target accounts, salespeople invest time with buyers in accounts most likely to convert into sales and most relevant to convert, with the messaging most likely to do so.

The reasons that it is challenging for most salespeople to make these types of data driven decisions—that maximizes return on sales resources invested—are that they don't have the data access, analytical capabilities, or time to do so. They are going on gut feeling most of the time instead and going with face-to-face meetings by default rather than assessing whether a virtual meeting would have been a better fit for the situation.

Generic sales plays are not fit for different customer meetings with different objectives

Most salespeople who have gone through basic sales training know the right thing to do to make customer interactions count. Identify the opportunity the customer is missing out on and the action they should take to address it.

The format of this customer contact is an assumed value proposition, investigative questions and a call-to-action. What this format requires is two things from the selling part's side: A set of standardized sales plays in the form of "if you do x and think you would be able to achieve y, because of a, b, c," and time to prepare sales plays tailored to different customer interactions.

It is rare that the sales rep doesn't know that leading with value and a clear call-to-action is the right approach to increase the probability of the meeting converting into sales, but more often that, with responsibility for hundreds of accounts and 3–5 customer meetings per day they don't have the time to do it.

Because of the lack of time, they end up with ineffective generic sales plays instead that do not fit the customer and are unlikely to be effective at converting time invested in the meeting into sales.

Too little time to focus on their most important accounts	There are two problems with giving transactional sales reps larger account portfolios than they can handle, and that is absolutely the case if they have hundreds of accounts. Smaller accounts with lower total purchase value and potential end up being overserved and larger accounts with high purchase value and potential end up being underserved.
	The long tail 80% of customers that only accounts for 20% of sales ends up taking half of the sales rep's time. Not necessarily because the sales rep plans it this way, but more often as a consequence of having the responsibility for also accommodating requests from and managing these smaller accounts which takes away time from growing business with the bigger and higher potential accounts.
	In one building materials manufacturer we were working with we found that at year-end, over 25% of the accounts deemed high potential based on data had not received a single interaction, because 40% of time was spent reactively accommodating requests from lower importance ones
Inability to identify new potential high importance accounts due to poor intelligence	Even if the sales reps were able to allocate sufficient time to their most important accounts, the way they most typically decide who is important now is based on who has historically been important in the past.
	The problem is that companies change and some grow to become highly important, but the sales rep might not have registered this and therefore doesn't allocate time to these ones.

To address these challenges about the lack of time for customer engagement, who time is allocated to and how it is spent, leaders of sales teams with a transactional selling model consider the following four complementary roles:

TRANSACTIONAL SELLING MODEL—COMPLEMENTARY ROLES

1. Data analyst

Role with expertise in gathering, structuring, and setting up continuous analysis of data, to (a) identify sales activity and resultant causality patterns and (b) making ongoing recommendations on which accounts show relevance to invest time in to grow sales and what the focus of those interactions should be.

The data analyst can take responsibility for providing the team with data-driven recommendations on how to maximize sales return on time invested in the portfolio of existing and potential target accounts and make those recommendations better over time. Additionally, the data analyst can take responsibility for developing the data visualizations in the form of dashboards, used by the sales team for ongoing decision-making and for saving time on preparation by sales reps before customer meetings.

The data analyst enables the team as a whole to make better and faster decisions through an objective perspective on how the team should best invest its limited time for customer engagement with a large portfolio of accounts.

2. Sales planner and playmaker

Role with expertise in planning, organization, and communication to help customer facing sales reps get time booked in with the right accounts, at the right times, and with the right focus for the interaction. They increase sales efficiency through time saved for the sales rep, and sales effectiveness through of the sales reps spending a higher share of customer meetings with high relevance accounts around topics most likely to convert to sales. They take insights prepared by the data analyst, prioritize which identified opportunities are most relevant to act on now, prepare different sales plays to run on the prioritized opportunities, and activate sales reps, either sharing sales play recommendations with them or booking meetings for them directly.

The sales planner and playmaker is able to take responsibility for continuously recommending or directly booking sales meetings for the sales reps that are identified as high relevance based on data and preparing the focus and contents of the conversation most likely to drive sales. If the analysis of account data and activity shows high relevance for a meeting to discuss opportunity x with account y, the sales planner and playmaker takes initiative to follow up to either recommend a concrete sales play for the rep to run or directly book the meeting on behalf of the sales rep.

The purpose of the sales planner and playmaker isn't to tell the sales reps what to do, but rather to enable the sales reps to get more time for customer facing activities and get more value out of those activities. This is why most companies implementing this role on the sales team typically start with having them recommend activities and meetings that the sales reps can decide to use or not and then progressing toward directly booking meetings in the sales reps' calendars later on.

3. Inside sales rep

Role with expertise in remote customer engagement through digital and virtual channels to take responsibility for managing incoming leads from marketing, customer purchase order handling, and management of business with smaller, lower importance accounts, where the potential sales returns of customer interactions do not justify them being face-to-face.

The inside sales rep on the transactional selling team can take responsibility for the selling tasks that could or should be done fully remotely, thus freeing up sales rep time so they can focus on customer engagement with those accounts most likely to drive sales growth. Inside sales reps qualify and convert incoming leads generated by marketing and manage customer order requests. They act as account managers for lower-value customers instead of sales reps having this responsibility.

The purpose of the inside sales rep is to reduce sales rep time spent on customers and interactions assessed to yield a low return on sales time invested, to grow the entire team's sales efficiency and effectiveness. It is not that lower-value accounts that the inside sales rep would be responsible for could never get a physical meeting, it is just that the default mode should be that they don't.

4. Demand generation specialist

Role with expertise in creating and implementing demand generation programs towards the team's target customer segments to drive demand for the company's offering. The demand generation specialist on the team can take responsibility for generating leads and purchasing order requests, through digital engagement with the team's target customer segment and stakeholders.

The purpose of the demand generation specialist is to take advantage of the fact that the team's target customers use both digital and analogue channels to get inspired, engage with—and buy from the vendors they work with.

The formula for transactional *Teams That Sell* is

(quantity of customer engagements) x (quality of customers) x (quality of interactions) = success

and a team-based approach to selling in these types of organizations grows sales efficiency and effectiveness by improving all three factors that drive sales growth and profitability in their business.

Take the example of VELUX, the global leader in roof window solutions for buildings. One of the important routes to market for the company is through the carpenters, roofers, and building companies that buy the product from dealers and install it in the projects they are working on. The problem is that there are tens of thousands of these types of companies in a typical market, ranging from small one-man-bands to large professional enterprises. To focus the company's experienced sales reps on interactions with high relevance accounts, assessed to yield the highest return on time invested, inside sales reps are used to take responsibility for the long tail of lower importance accounts and to guide both sales reps and inside sales reps on who to allocate time to and what to focus on in those interactions, after a playmaker recommends sales plays based on data and analysis.

For a company like VELUX, or other companies with similar characteristics of lower complexity sales and value realized from the product performance rather than business adoption and adaption, this approach grows sales efficiency and effectiveness, leading to higher growth for lower cost in sales. Having *Teams That Sell* in place for these types of companies also ensures that leaders have a system in place, beyond the sales individual, to help new hires get up to performance more rapidly, thus reducing the challenge of high turnover rates in the salesforce.

THE CONSULTATIVE SALES TEAM

Sales organizations characterized by lower complexity sales, where the value of the offering comes from business adoption and adaption of the product, rather than the performance of the product itself, have become synonymous with one type of company: SaaS.

- They have lower complexity solutions to sell and buy because there are fewer stakeholders involved in the average purchase, and the solution being bought is more standardized and, seen from a financial perspective, comes with lower risk.

- The value of the solution is only realized with user adoption and adaption of their ways of working.

Although SaaS companies dominate the type of selling that is characterized by lower complexity sales and value realization from organizational adoption, we don't call this type of sales 'SaaS selling' for two reasons:

- SaaS companies deliver value through adoption by the organization, but not all of these are low complexity to sell. Take Showpad or Salesforce.com as examples, who sell higher priced solutions that involves a high number of technical and business stakeholders to buy.

- Not all companies with lower sales complexity and value realization from adoption are SaaS companies. Companies like Lego Education sell physical teaching tools to educational institutions, which are only valuable if used continuously and used correctly by their organization.

Instead, we call it consultative sales because unlike enterprise sales that need to address a broad range of business stakeholders to get bought, these types of solutions are targeted towards a narrower buying audience of a specific function in the business to address a specific set of functional challenges.

Some examples include Contractbook for sales, Lego Education for educators, and Hubspot for Marketing.

Sales organizations characterized by consultative sales have in common a shared blueprint for how they drive growth in their businesses, following a *land and expand* philosophy with five engines that operate sequentially:

LAND AND EXPAND BLUEPRINT

Demand engine
They create awareness and interest through digital marketing or direct outreach to attract target buyers to digital points of self-education and conversation, such as a website landing page. **The demand engine** is responsible for generating awareness and interest with the company's target buyers in both the challenges its solution solves and the solution itself.

Lead Engine
They capture and convert qualified leads to opportunities to initiate the dialogue and buying process with relevant companies and stakeholders.

Deal Engine
They move opportunities to closure through a multiphase sales process centered around conversations to (1) diagnose pain, potential, and requirements, (2) demonstrate the solution and value, and (3) close a contract, with a **deal engine** responsible for converting qualified opportunities into closed contracts with new customers.

Customer Success Engine
They onboard new customers to reduce customer churn after signing and deliver the customer value required to expand business engagement, with a **customer onboarding engine** responsible for driving customer adoption of the solution.

Account Development Engine
They develop existing customers to grow the sales volume and the scope of offerings bought by buyers, with an **account development engine** responsible for growing customer contract value over time.

Get them interested→Get them started→Get them growing→Keep them loyal.

Unlike enterprise sales, where it is difficult to talk about a *standardized* sales process because of the high variation in the number of stakeholders involved and the uniqueness of each customer buying process, consultative selling is exactly about identifying the recipe that most effectively and efficiently converts market potential into new customers and grows these customers over time. Because of the narrower target audience and solution scope compared to enterprise sales, the commercial leaders responsible for consultative selling focus on defining a replicable playbook for customer acquisition and development that best works for their target audience and solution, putting it into operation, and continuously improving it.

This is the reason why most sales organizations with a consultative selling model are in fact not set up with individual sales reps with broad responsibility for everything from prospecting and opportunity management to customer on-boarding and account development. Instead, most use a factory setup, where specialist teams work sequentially, each with their own area of responsibility along the customer journey.

- **The demand generation team** is responsible for generating awareness and interest with the company's target buyers in the challenges its solution solves and the solution itself. Consisting of marketing specialists, this team is ultimate measured on their ability to generate pipeline value for sales and the percent win rate of these opportunities.

- **The prospecting and lead qualification team** is responsible for generating pipeline value for sales through its own prospecting and initial contact with incoming leads to qualify and convert them. Consisting of BDRs, this team is measured on their ability to book meetings for the company's salespeople, the percent share of those meetings that convert to sales, and the value of those deals.

- **The deal team** is responsible for generating new business sales by converting qualified leads into closed sales through a series of conversations with the buyer, from needs identification and solution demonstration to negotiation and close. Consisting of SDRs or account executives (AEs), this team is measured on their ability to generate new business sales with customer acquisition accounts.

- **The customer success team** is responsible for getting new customers successfully started using the solution, getting value from it at an operational level, and expanding their use of the solution when needed. Consisting of customer success managers, the team is measured on their ability to grow customer solution usage to prevent churn and create new opportunities for sales on existing accounts.

- **The account management team** is responsible for growing the scale (number of units bought) and scope (types of offerings bought) of the business engagement with existing customers and keep them buying. Consisting of AEs, the team is measured on their ability to grow sales to existing accounts and percent churn-rate on the accounts they are responsible for.

Teams of individual specialists working sequentially in a factory setup are great for three things: efficiency, with specialist roles on each team focused on executing a narrow set of tasks with minimal coordination costs; scalability, with separate engines to drive different elements of new customer acquisition and account growth that can be quickly set up and grown by hiring more specialists; predictability in a stable business environment, with each engine continuously contributing their part to make the growth machinery work as a whole.

Although these advantages of a factory setup for consultative selling fit well with SaaS companies' need for rapid scaling, having teams of individual specialists that work sequentially comes with its own set of challenges for leaders responsible for sales organization characterized by a consultative selling model. Those challenges include the following:

CONSULTATIVE SELLING MODEL—RISKS

Silo optimization in specialist teams is efficient but leads to overall commercial ineffectiveness:

The big benefit of the factory setup where specialist teams work sequentially along the buying and account development journey is that it allows for high efficiency in each specialist engine. The demand generation team can focus only on churning out a high number of leads. The presales team can focus on churning out a high number of meetings for the deal team. And so on.

The risk, however, is that siloed optimization in each specialist team leads to ineffectiveness of the commercial engine overall. The classic examples are when the demand generation team generates a high number of low-quality leads, making the presales team ineffective because high time spent on lead qualification or the presales team booking a high number of meetings with the wrong people, making the deal team ineffective.

To address this challenge, commercial leaders with a factory setup in these types of organizations typically implement shared KPIs and collaboration mechanisms between different specialist teams to drive alignment, rather than getting them on the same team where the organizational design gives them this directly.

An efficient process is seen from the sales perspective, but not from the customer's:

For anyone who has ever tried being a part of large telecom customer service company or had a case in the public sector will recognize when processes have been designed *inside-out*, with little consideration for what this does to the customer's experience: being handed over from one person to another, because each sit with their own little part of the entire process.

A factory setup scales well but is slow to change:

While the big benefit of a factory setup is how it can drive high efficiency gains for less complex standardized processes (like Ford producing cars through 84 steps on a conveyer belt in the 1930s), the challenge is that these kinds of setups are inflexible to changes their environment and in how they need to operate. If the customer onboarding team is struggling with high customer drop-off rates for new customers, because of the poor fit customer types being sold to, the whole machinery needs to change in the previous specialist teams to address this challenge. As a result, change takes a long time.

By design, the factory setup for commercial operations

drives high process efficiency through specialized teams working sequentially, with the success of one team highly dependent on how well and what the others do. The trade-off is that with this higher dependency between different teams comes higher complexity when making changes, because a change in one part of the machinery will influence the entire system.

To address this challenge in factory setups, commercial leaders typically to set up a revenue operations or operational commercial excellence function, where people are employed to look at the machinery end-to-end, rather than breaking the big machine into smaller machines.

There are high employee turnover rates: Employee turnover rates are high in sales, averaging 30% replacement per year compared to 13% for companies on average, but even higher for SaaS sales at 35%.[40]

Although part of the higher employee turnover rates in sales is likely caused by the *perform or out* nature of the profession, and for SaaS specifically perhaps because of younger employees, the problem for sales leaders is that a 5% increase in sales rep turnover rates are estimated to increase selling costs by 4–6% and reduce overall revenue attainment rates by 2–3%.[41]

Part of the explanation is however also likely found in the factory setup itself, used by many SaaS sales organizations to organize labor. While only 8% of people who are set up to work individually are engaged in their work, that number jumps five times to 45% for people working in teams with a team leader they trust.[42]

A team-based way of working drives employee engagement that lowers employee turnover rates.

For sales leaders responsible for consultative selling organizations, typically organized into a factory setup of specialist teams working sequentially with each team member working individually, the question regarding *Teams That Sell* is

40. https://www.xactlycorp.com/blog/sales-turnover-statistics

41. https://www.forbes.com/sites/stephendiorio/2021/11/16/the-growing-talent-crisis-in-sales/?sh=545db1f665c5

42. adp_the-power-of-hidden-teams-reprint_20190906.ashx

How can I grow the effectiveness of the sales organization as a whole by creating teams of people with complementary capabilities that work together towards a shared objective of growing sales with a specific target customer segment?

COMPLIMENTARY ROLES TO MAKE CONSULTATIVE SELLING MORE EFFECTIVE

The organizational shift for leaders with responsibility for consultative selling is typically less about hiring a lot of new specialist roles, and more about whether those specialist roles they already have should be divided to work in separate teams or put on the same team.

Rather than having demand generation, prospecting, presale, and deal teams working sequentially, put marketing specialists, BDRs, SDRs, and AEs on the same team, with a common goal of growing a specific target customer segment.

Rather than having customer on-boarding, customer success, and account management teams working separately, put customer on-boarding specialists, customers success managers, and account managers together to collaborate around growing business engagement within existing accounts.

Create mini factories instead of a mega factory.

Collaborate around growing business engagement within existing accounts.

From different research about SaaS sales specifically, we have a fairly good idea about what each of these *Teams That Sell* need to do to be successful:

CONSULTATIVE SELLING MODEL—BEST PRACTICE CHARACTERISTICS

A simple and easy buying process

In one study[43] of business-to-business SaaS buyers, what was ranked as most important when buying these kinds of offerings was a "short, quick, and flawless buying process." Of the respondents in the survey, 44% also ranked "too complex sales process" as a top-three reason for salespeople losing a sale.

Making it easy for buyers to move through their decision process towards final purchasing decision is key for this simpler type selling.

Teams That Sell in consultative selling need to avoid the constant handover process of customers that a factory setup of specialist teams working sequentially can suffer from to deliver a low friction buying experience for the buyers they engage with.

Maximize selling time with buyers who have a need

In the same study, 49% of business-to-business SaaS buyers ranked "no fit with business need" as the number one reason that led to a lost sale during the sales process they were engaged in.

Spending time selling to people who are not interested in buying because the offering does not fit with their business needs is a great sales efficiency killer because it takes away time that could be spent on people who actually need the offering.

Teams That Sell need to ensure that the people on the team take responsibility for engaging with decision-makers to help them buy and maximize the time they spend with people who actually have a need to get the problem solved through the solution they purchased (and avoid trying to sell to people who are not interested in buying).

Buyer education and enablement

Modern buyers self-educate, not only before starting a formal buying process but also while they are in process with a vendor and once they become customers. For sales in general, buyers spend more than four times as much time researching independently and meeting internally than meeting with vendors during their buying process.[44]

Teams That Sell need to ensure that potential and existing customers are continuously educated and enabled through other channels than direct personal engagement, to most effectively start and drive the buying processes forward.

Business over product focus	Top performing sales reps working with consultative sales spend 39% less time talking about technical topics and products features, compared to average performers and spend 23% more time discussing business-topic questions.[45] Because consultative selling is less about product performance (like in technical sales) and more about what that product enables the organization to do differently and achieve, the focus of the team should be on the customer's business, with the offering as an enabler. Demonstrating business value is especially important when selling to people lower in the organization, with a greater need to equip them with a strong business case for making the purchase. For people at the manager or director level, this is the number one requirement for consultative sales vendors.[46]
	Teams That Sell need to set up the people on the team with responsibility for engaging with decision-makers to help them buy, and to have a conversation about the buyer's business and business case for adopting the solution.
Offer a personalized buying experience with a real person (not a salesperson)	From research at one consultative selling company (Hubspot) about the traits of high performing salespeople,[47] we know that characteristics like preparation, adaptability, domain expertise, intelligence, and passion matter. More classical sales characteristics like objection handling, convincing, or closing ability are negatively correlated with success. Conversation mastery matters.
	Teams That Sell need people as their points of contact with customers—people who aren't instructed to blindly follow conversation scripts and templates but rather equipped with the understanding and ability to navigate actual human conversations.
Help customers proactively identify and address challenges and opportunities	Fast growing companies with consultative selling models are 43% more likely to invest in customer success programs than average,[48] because a land-and-expand approach to growing sales demands high emphasis on customer success.
	Teams That Sell need to not only enable the customer to buy their offering, but also enable the customer's business to get the product successfully integrated into their operations, and then use that success as the point of departure for proactively identifying new possibilities for value creation through expansion of use.

43. https://www.walnut.io/post/what-saas-buyers-really-want

44. https://www.gartner.com/en/sales/insights/b2b-buying-journey

45. https://www.gong.io/blog/sales-leaderboard/

46. https://www.walnut.io/post/what-saas-buyers-really-want

48. https://blog.hubspot.com/service/customer-success-business-success

In the transition from a mega factory to smaller collaborative teams with the complementary capabilities to drive growth on their own, sales leaders effectively take many of the roles divided into specialist teams and group them together around a common objective: to grow sales. Just as with other types of *Teams That Sell*, the purpose of getting different specialist roles on the same team, rather working individually with broad or narrow individual responsibility, is to make the whole more than the sum of its individual parts and grow sales, effectiveness, and efficiency. These specialist roles include the following:

> The purpose of getting different specialist roles on the same team, is to make the whole more than the sum of its individual parts.

CONSULTATIVE SELLING MODEL—COMPLEMENTARY ROLES

1. Account executive

An AE has expertise in buyer engagement to activate and drive forward buying processes with potential and existing buyers. They are hired to help new potential customers move from interested to buying decision and help existing customers understand and address new opportunities for value creation through increased use of the vendor's offering. They engage in interactions with key decision-makers to help explore the potential value of starting to adopt their offering or expanding their existing use, converting interest to intention, and interactions to demonstrate how the solution in scope works and how it could help the customer's company work better, converting intention to determination. They also interact to present the proposal and get a final purchasing decision, converting determination into a final decision.

What the AE can do better than the rest is manage conversations with key decision-makers about their business to guide them forward in their decision process. This is why The AE should be equipped with the key skills of conversation mastery and the ability to relate the solution in scope to the customer's business in terms of use and value. The AE needs a team to help them maximize the time they spend on the type of customer engagement they are hired for and to make sure that time is spent with the right people and accounts on the right topics.

Although the sales leader could decide to further specialize account executives into either a customer acquisition or an account development focus, the responsibility of the role is essentially the same—to engage with customer decision-makers to drive sales.

2. Sales development rep

An SDR has expertise in buyer engagement to generate and capture interest, to create sales-qualified leads and pipeline value for the team. These people are hired to convert market potential into sales potential for the AE for work on in the early stages of the customer's buying process. They reach out directly to target potential customers to generate and qualify interest and the ability to buy. Responding to leads captured through digital touchpoints, they qualify and convert these leads through research on and conversation with the potential customer. SDRs enrich sales-qualified leads with additional information that is valuable for the AE in their initial engagement with the potential customer. They continue the handover of leads assessed mature enough to the team's AE.

What the SDR does best is identify accounts and contacts that fit the company's ideal customer and buyer profiles and engage with these to create high win-rate pipeline value for the team's AEs to work on. They bridge between market potential (in the form of target accounts or captured leads) and sales potential (in the form of qualified sales opportunities). Because this role does not require expertise in the customer's business or conversation mastery to the same extent as the AE, the sales leader can typically hire more junior people with high intelligence and passion for this role, who can then progress into AE roles over time as their experience grows.

Although the sales leader could decide to further specialize the SDR function into even more narrow areas of responsibility like research and data gathering, prospecting, or lead management to maximize efficiency of performing these tasks, we must be aware of the potential effect on employee engagement and turnover rates of doing so. It is better to create a versatile and meaningful job where the SDR conducts different tasks to achieve the same objective: Pipeline value for the team that converts into new sales.

3. Digital marketing specialist

This specialist has expertise in digital and content marketing to activate and drive forward the customer buying journeys through digital touchpoints. This person is hired to take responsibility for building, running, and improving on the marketing programs that use digital channels to engage with the team's potential and existing target customers and help them forward in their decision-making process. They are responsible for digital marketing programs to create awareness and interest with prospective customers, to increase leads generated for the team, ensure the quality of leads generated and the success-rate when SDRs reach out. They create digital marketing programs to enable buyer self-education while they are going through a formal buying process with an AE from the team, to ease the process, make it shorter, and achieve higher win-rates, as well as digital marketing programs to help existing customers understand new opportunities for value creation, based on their use of the offering and digital activity, to create new opportunities for growing account value. They also create digital marketing programs to prevent churn and increase loyalty.

The digital marketing specialist can create tracks of digital customer engagement that complement the team's direct engagement through its AEs, SDRs or customer success managers in a world where buyers use both digital and direct channels throughout their buying journey. This specialist targets prospective customers that SDRs then reach out to, having already been primed through digital engagement. They simultaneously digitally enable and nurture qualified opportunities that sales executives are working on directly. Existing customers that AEs and customer success managers are working with receive digital nurturing at the same time to create new opportunities for expanding business engagement. Because this role is not limited to generating new customer acquisition leads for SDRs, the team leader needs to hire specialists with the ability to understand customer buying and development journeys and how digital engagement would best complement sales and customer success activities to drive growth.

Although leaders could decide to reduce the scope of the digital marketing specialist to generating contacts for sales roles to work on (lead gen), this ignores the fact that buyers and customers use digital channels not only to become aware and interested initially, but also throughout their entire journey to their first purchase and beyond. To have digital engagement in place that complements the work of the sales roles end-to-end, the digital marketing specialist is brought onto the team for alignment between digital and direct buyer engagement and given broader responsibility for growing sales through new customer acquisition and account development.

4. Customer success manager

Technical and operational specialist with responsibility for growing customer adoption of solutions bought in operations, to help customers realize value from their purchases and help the team create new opportunities for expanding business engagement with customers. They are hired to engage with the customer at an operational level to make sure potential customers understand how the solution works and creates value in customer operations, to help new customers get started and ongoing customers are enabled to expand the value they get out of working with their company over time. They give solution demonstrations and go through post-purchase adoption plans during the new customer acquisition process.

These managers conduct trainings with users in new customers' organizations and deliver front-line support to solve customer challenges that hold back value realization. They identify new opportunities for customer value creation by expanding use of the company's offering that can be addressed by the AE with decision-makers in the customer's organization.

What the customer success manager does best is engage with the customer at an operational level to proactively drive forward adoption of the solution in customer operations. As a complement to the AE, this manager is focused on engagement with the customer's business decision-makers, which is especially important for a type of selling characterized by the value of the offering coming from business adoption and adaption, rather than the performance of the product itself. The customer success manager is such an important part of the team that some companies even regard the manager as part of the offering and charge for their service. In addition to strong technical understanding of their offering and the customer's operations where they need to drive adoption, great customers success managers need strong change management skills. They set adoption goals with the customer, identify main barriers to achieving those goals (lack of understanding why adoption matters for them, or missing the ability to use the solution), and conduct activities with customer stakeholders to address these issues. Once one adoption goal has been reached a new one is set to unlock additional value, sometimes requiring the customer to expand on solution purchasing to reach this goal. At that point, the AE comes in to play. The customer success manager grows the average account value and reduces customer churn by continuously growing the value customers receive from being a customer.

While the team leader could choose to further specialize customer success managers into focusing on different parts of the customer buying and development journey, such as a product demonstration specialist, new customer onboarding specialist, or account development specialist, this is likely to result in a poorer customer experience through being handed from one customer success manager to the other. The price for higher efficiency in individual task execution is likely poorer performance overall caused by a worse customer experience and higher employee turnover in the customer success role because of task fatigue.

Although these are the core roles with operational responsibility for growing sales from the team's target customer segment, these are not necessarily the only roles involved in growing efficiency and effectiveness in how the team sells. The revenue operations function of these types of sales organizations continues to play a central role in enabling the teams to continually improve through the insights they gain.

In addition to the team leader, the core of the consultative *Teams That Sell* is

- the AE, who takes responsibility for direct customer engagement at the business level to drive sales opportunities forward and grow business engagement with existing accounts;

- the SDR, who takes responsibility for direct engagement with target accounts to create new sales opportunities and pipeline value for the team;

- the digital marketing specialist, who takes responsibility for digital engagement that activates and drives forward customer acquisition and account development;

- and the customer success manager, who takes responsibility for operational engagement to grow solution adoption and value realized for the customer.

Take the example of SMART Technologies mentioned in the beginning of this book:[49] selling interactive displays and software to educators and educational institutions. Rather than continuing with a factory setup where functional specialist teams worked sequentially, the company has shifted to what they call *unified commercial engines*, where complementary roles from marketing, sales, and customer success are joined to collaborate around growing sales within a specific customer segment.

This allows SMART Technologies, and similar organizations with a consultative selling model, to not only grow overall sales and sales

---

49. https://www.smarttech.com/

efficiency, as demonstrated in the case, but also to create a better place to work for the people working in their commercial organization by setting them up less as cogwheels on a conveyer belt and more as humans that work together to help more of their target customers get more value from their offering.

> Create a better place
> to work for the people
> working in their commercial
> organization by setting them
> up less as cogwheels on a
> conveyer belt and more as
> humans that work together.

The questions that however still remain are; what customer segments different teams should have responsibility for and how many are needed, but before getting into how we answer that, there is one last type of *Teams That Sell* to cover:

Those that don't sell directly to customers, but to, through, or with others.

THE PARTNER SALES TEAM

In addition to technical, enterprise, transactional, and consultative selling, there is one last selling type to cover that is different from the first four types in one particular way: the sales organization that doesn't sell directly to customers, but rather takes their offerings to market through others, who then sell it to their customers.

> The sales organization that doesn't sell directly to customers, but rather takes their offerings to market through others, who then sell it to their customers.

These sales are partner sales, whether it be through agents, distributors, or other types of stakeholders.

Whereas the key question for the first four selling types centered around how to most effectively drive their customers' specific buying and development journeys forward directly, partner sales are unique in how the commercial organization best enables, motivates, and incentivizes other to start—and drive customer buying journeys forward.

Although it is challenging to say exactly how this is best done, because partners can vary greatly regarding the type of selling they need to succeed with, those that do it well generally have five things in common:

PARTNER SALES—EXPERTISES

Partner portfolio selection and management	They make sure to select the right partners that have the greatest ability and interest in growing sales of their offering, and continuously assess their partner portfolio against alternatives to ensure it is optimized to drive growth throughout.
Contract creation and management	They have a strong ability to negotiate contracts with partners that ensure incentives and disincentives are in place to encourage partners to sell their offering and proactively addresses deviations from agreed contact volumes.
Partner sales enablement	Help partners succeed with customer selling activities related to their offering, by generating leads for them, equipping them with insights, content, and digital partner self-service tools and support on specific deals when required.
Partner relationship management and education	They build trust with selected partners over time and continuously educate partners on their customers, offering category, and specific products and services.
Purchasing order and customer service request handling	They enable partners to easily place orders, get them processed, and get support handling ad-hoc problems which may arise related to the offering they are selling.

Partner selling is perhaps best understood as an ongoing change management process, where the commercial organization selling to, through, or with selected partners is responsible for implementing a system of activities that continuously creates the awareness, desire, knowledge, ability, and reinforcement required to motivate and enable others to take action to grow sales.

The most typical way of organizing successful selling around partner sales is an island setup where individual sales reps are given responsibility for growing sales with a portfolio of partners in a given segment and geographical area and are supported by channel marketing and customer service functions.

While the specific activities of the individual partner sales rep can vary greatly depending on the size and type of the partner(s) they are responsible for—which can be everything from a portfolio of hundreds of partners to a single one—partner sales reps are typically hired for their ability to do four things:

PARTNER SELLING MODEL—ACTIVITIES

Partner relationship management	The team engages in ongoing interactions with different stakeholders in the partner's organization to strengthen relationships that the sales professional is dependent on to get their offering to market through the partner.
Contract management	They have ongoing interactions with key decision-makers in the partner's organization to discuss potential gaps between estimated and actual sales volumes through the partner and agree on actions required to close these gaps.
Partner business development	They have ongoing interactions with key decision-makers in the partner's organization to help them grow sales of the existing portfolio of products and services they sell and adopt new ones into their portfolio of offerings for their customers.
Partner portfolio management	They prospect for new potential partners and replacing existing ones if necessary, to best reach final end-customers of their products and services and drive sales growth and margin improvements.

Essentially each partner sales rep has responsibility for driving sales of their company's offerings to their own specific customer segment and geography by developing and managing a portfolio of external partners. The partner sales rep can best manage engagement with a portfolio of selected partners (and the key stakeholders in these) to get new potential partners to start selling and motivate, incentivize, and enable existing ones to sell more.

However, just as for salespeople in organizations with other types of selling models, being set up to work alone comes with its own set of challenges, including four in particular for partner selling:

PARTNER SELLING MODEL—CHALLENGES

Too little time for partner relationship and business development activities that create new sales: Despite the fact that most companies working with a partner sales model have implemented some form of partner self-service portal for purchasing order handling, like e-commerce, the dominant form of placing orders is still via e-mail[50] and often through the partner sales rep they are accustomed to work with. The challenge is that although order taking and handling is of course important, it takes away time for the agent sales rep to focus on the activities with their partners that generate this order flow to begin with.

Partner sales training is critical but time consuming: Just as companies train their own salespeople on how to sell their offerings to their target customers, partner sales organizations need to ensure their partners' salespeople are equipped with the knowledge required to take their offering to market on their behalf. The challenge is that people training is time consuming and in many partner sales organizations, it is left to the partner sales rep to take care of, taking away time from engaging with stakeholders at the business level to develop the business with the partner.

Lack of insights required to make ideal decisions at the level of the individual partner and the overall partner portfolio: To best grow sales through portfolio of partners, partner sales reps continuously need to ask and answer three questions at the individual account level in their portfolio:

- *What potential deviations from estimated sales in the contract need to be addressed and what is causing these deviations?*

- *What are the most ideal new offerings to expand partner business engagement with?*

- *Who are the new relevant stakeholders in the partner's organization that I need to motivate, incentivize, and enable to sell our offerings?*

Similarly, the partner sales rep needs to ensure that the portfolio partners they choose to work with are the ones most ideal to drive sales through. The challenge is that while all partner sales

	reps make these decisions, few do so based on the structured research and analysis required to ensure good decision-making at the individual and partner portfolio level. This leaves the partner sales rep in a reactive rather than proactive mode. They are not in control of driving sales, but rather reacting to it.
Channel marketing activities are not aligned to selling activities:	Because of their role as a sales enabler, marketing is perhaps especially important when it comes to partner selling, where both partners commercial organizations need to be enabled to sell and the partner sales reps of their own organization need to be enabled to drive sales through their partners. The challenge is that most often these channel marketers work in a centralized function, creating alignment problems between their own activities in events, content creation, or lead management and those of the partner sales reps they need to enable.

For the commercial leader responsible for getting their offering to market through a partner sales model, the key question around moving from teams of individual partner sales reps to teams that conduct partner selling is this:

How do I enable partner sales reps to maximize time spent on partner relationships and business development activities and enable them to get the most out of this time and the portfolio partners they choose to work with?

How do I enable partner sales reps to maximize time spent on partner relationships?

50. https://goautonomous.io

COMPLEMENTARY ROLES TO MAKE PARTNER SELLING MORE EFFECTIVE THROUGH A TEAM THAT DRIVES SALES

The organizational shift for commercial leaders responsible for partner selling models is typically one of getting both existing roles in the company onto the same operating team as the partner sales reps and considering a few additional roles to make the division of labor more effective.

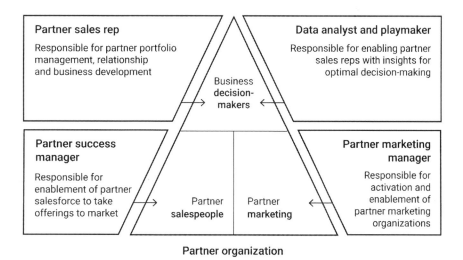

*Figure 14: **Partner Sales Teams.***
Four roles to drive sales through the team's partner portfolio.

PARTNER SELLING MODEL—COMPLEMENTARY ROLES

1. Partner Success Manager

This sales enablement specialist is responsible for engaging with the partner's organization at an operational level to help equip relevant people in the partners' commercial organizations with the knowledge, skills, and content required to sell their offering. This role is like the customer success managers of an enterprise or consultative selling model, who assess how mature the partner is and conduct activities with people in their organization to drive forward adoption. This manager trains salespeople in new partner organizations to understand their products and services, their benefits, and how to discuss them with customers. They demonstrate new products to the partners' salespeople as well as the supporting content and sales assets that go with it. They follow up on leads handed over to the partner's sales organization or manage customer purchasing requests.

What the customer success manager does best is to engage with the customer at an operational level, to proactively drive forward adoption of the solution in customer operations. This manager acts as a complement to the partner sales rep, focused on engagement with the customer's business decision-makers, which is especially important for a type of selling characterized by the partner business's willingness to invest their organization in growing sales. The partner success manager helps the sales team accomplish two things: Freeing up time for the partner sales rep to focus on developing the relationship and business engagement with the partner's business decision makers, while at the same time growing sales through each partner by enabling each partner's organization to successfully take their offering to market

2. Data analyst and playmaker

This research and analysis specialist is responsible for equipping partner sales reps with the insights they need for four decision types in their work managing individual partners and a portfolio of partners: (1) insights about sales deviations from estimated contract volumes and potential causes of this with individual partners, used in interactions with partner business stakeholders to proactively address potential barriers to take their offering to market, (2) insights about partner's existing purchasing volumes and patterns and recommendations about ideal next offerings the partner should start selling, used in business development discussions with partner's business decision-makers, (3) insights about changes to the partner's commercial organization, used by both the partner sales rep and partner success manager to plan engagement with new relevant stakeholders, and (4) insights about new potential partners in the designated customer segment and geography that the team should either consider adding to the portfolio of partners or use to replace existing nonperforming partners in the portfolio.

The data analyst and playmaker is able to help the team make better decisions about what they do with different partners in their portfolio and who they decide to invest in building and managing partnerships with. They become proactive and take control of the activities and actions they see as most likely to drive sales with the segment and geography they are responsible for, rather than just reacting to partner requests.

3. Partner marketing manager

This channel marketing specialist is responsible for engaging with the partners' marketing organizations to help them embed relevant content, assets, and campaigns into each partners' own commercial activities and ensuring the team's partner success managers and partner sales reps are enabled to conduct theirs. They are also responsible for an annual marketing planning meeting with each partner's marketing organization to ensure inclusion of activities supporting sales of their offering. They enable partner marketing organizations to put content and insights to use with their front-line salespeople. They carry out the planning and execution of activities (such as events) for partner portfolio development in the segment and geography their team is responsible for. They activate and enable partner sales reps to take new offerings to their portfolio of partners in business development discussions.

The partner marketing manager is able to help ensure that selling in the partner organization is not only happening through the partner's salesforce, but also driven through marketing activities, and to ensure that their own team is enabled with marketing activities that help them drive sales through the partner portfolio.

What this team of specialists can do, that partner sales reps working alone will struggle with, is to engage with the partner organization at the business-decision level, salesforce level, and marketing level to drive growth through the partner. They use a mix of data and analytics capabilities from transactional sales, classical key account management from enterprise sales, and the customer success functions of SaaS companies.

Engaging with the partner organization at the business-decision level, salesforce level, and marketing level to drive growth through the partner.

KEY TAKEAWAYS

- Together with partner sales, there are five types of direct sales models commercial leaders use to take their offering to market, with the choice of which to use depending primarily on how complex the offering is to sell or buy, and the extent to which customer value comes from product performance or business adoption and adaption.

- Deciding which selling model is the best fit to get offerings to market matters because each has their own unique commercial activities to drive sales and commercial capabilities required to do so. The commercial leader needs to ensure that the organization is set up to deliver.

- There are five different types of *Teams That Sell* for the different types of selling that different companies need to succeed, because each of these vary regarding what needs to get done and the capabilities required to get it done. Each team comprises their own set of specialist roles with complementary capabilities required to grow sales and improve sales efficiency and effectiveness within the specific type of selling the team should use to succeed.

- Leaders of technical *Teams That Sell* typically hire salespeople with higher education technical backgrounds to take responsibility for engaging with key decision-makers during opportunity and account management, but are complemented by technical, inside sales and content marketing specialists to make selling most effective and cost efficient.

- Enterprise sales teams typically hire salespeople from business backgrounds as account executives to take responsibility for opportunity and account management, but complement them with sales playmakers, customer success managers and account-based marketing specialists, to make the team more effective at solving the complex tasks of customer acquisition and business development.

- Transactional sales teams typically hire salespeople with similar backgrounds as the professionals they are responsible for driving sales through, complemented by sales playmakers and planners, inside sales reps, and performance marketing specialists, to help teams maximize time with the right customers and stakeholders, at the right times, about the right things.

- A consultative sales team typically hires account executives to take responsibility for most new sales opportunities and account development, but complements them with sales development reps to take care of lower complexity selling tasks, customer success managers to help grow customer solution adoption, and digital marketing specialists to engage with existing and potential customers through digital channels.

- A partner sales team where partner account executives are complemented by partner success managers, data analysts, and a partner marketing manager, to make selling through others more effective.

- The value of shifting to all types of *Teams That Sell* is that they are able to make selling more efficient and effective, by taking advantage of specialists with different complementary capabilities and monetary compensation requirements to solve different selling tasks.

KEY QUESTIONS FOR COMMERCIAL LEADERSHIP

- **What type of selling do you need to excel at to take your offerings to market?** Are the products, services, and solutions you sell highly complex or simpler to buy and sell? Does the value come primarily from the performance of the product or from the customer adoption and adaption?

- **Do you have more than just one type of selling you need to succeed with?** Can all the selling you do be assigned to just one type of selling? Do you need to succeed with multiple types of selling for the offerings you have and the customers you take them to?

- **What kind of salespeople do you have today?** Do their characteristics fit with the types of selling that you need to succeed with?

- **What kind of complementary roles could make selling more efficient and effective?** What additional specialist roles do you believe could make the greatest impact on the efficiency and effectiveness of your sales organization if added to the teams? What tasks would they take ownership of and what should the existing sales professionals focus on instead?

"Talent wins games, but teamwork and intelligence win championships."

Michael Jordan

CHAPTER 3

ORGANIZING SALES INTO TEAMS THAT SELL

Key takeaway

Teams That Sell require a helix-organization where business value creation units (*Teams That Sell*) and expertise functions are intertwined, and the number of units required depends on the characteristics of the markets and customer segments they need to serve.

TEAMS THAT SELL NEED A HELIX ORGANIZATION

At the heart of *Teams That Sell* is the removal of functional specializations as the dominant organizing principle (teams of people that are the same and able to do the same), and replacing it with teams of people who have complementary capabilities required to collaborate around growing sales with a specific target customer group.

Instead of sales teams of salespeople with broad individual responsibility, sales teams of people with specialist areas of responsibility complement each other.

Instead of a mega factory setup of specialist teams with people working individually sequentially, set up mini factories with specialists joined to collaborate.

There is; however, a problem with replacing functional specialist teams with teams of complementary specialist roles. Because team members are no longer bound together by a shared functional expertise, but rather by a shared objective of how to most effectively grow sales towards their specific target customer segments, a new type of organizational setup is required, where value creation (what gets done on a day-to-day basis in the operational teams) is separated from functional best practice (how work gets done by specialist roles).

This is called the helix model,[51] which in essence is just a specific type of matrix organization that emphasizes clearly distinguishing between value creating units (where focus is on what gets done on a day-to-day basis), and functional excellence units (where focus is on how work gets done by individual people in those units).

- **Value creating units:** Where day-to-day work gets done by people who may have different capability specializations but collaborate around the achievement of shared goals and objectives. These are the *Teams That Sell*, led by team leaders responsible for making the team's operating model work, on a daily basis, to create value by growing sales with the team's target customer segment.

- **Functional excellence units:** Where best practice ways of working for different specialist roles is defined and specialist roles are hired and developed for them to be able to fill the role required on the operational teams they join. These are the functional communities, led by highly skilled, capability leaders, to ensure *Teams That Sell* are equipped with the different types of functional specialists required to make the team work as a whole.

---

51. https://www.mckinsey.com/capabilities/people-and-organizational-performance/our-insights/the-helix-organization

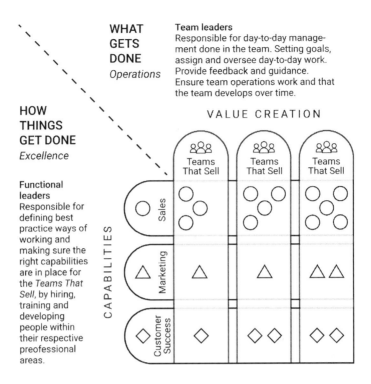

Figure 15: **The Helix Organisation for Teams That Sell.**
Value creation in operations and capability development in functions.

In a helix organization, functional specialists should belong to two types of teams, and report to two managers of equal, but different, relevance:

- **Value creation leaders:** These leaders are responsible for setting goals and managing day-to-day operations to deliver the goals through a team of people with different complementary capabilities.

- **Capability leaders**: These leaders are responsible for developing the company's capabilities within different functional specialist areas through best practice definition, hiring and firing, and people development.

Applied to *Teams That Sell*, the helix organization means that although functional expertise is being replaced by customer segments as the

151

dominant organizing principle in commercial operations, it does not mean the end of marketing, sales, or customer service functions.

People in *Teams That Sell* are hired into and developed professionally in the functional team of their professional specialization but operate on a day-to-day basis as part of a team with other types of specialists, sharing a specific customer segment focus, operating model, and goal of growing sales.

A commercial organization with a functional selling model of six *Teams That Sell*, focused on growing sales with different customer segments, will thus have six operational teams where value is created in terms of sales growth through customer acquisition and account development, where team members also belong to four functional groups representing the four different roles on the teams of AE, SDR, digital marketing specialists and customer success managers.

Although the helix organization serves as a good blueprint for how commercial leaders need to structure their organizations when moving from groups of individual specialists to *Teams That Sell*, one central question remains:

> *How should the value creating units (*Teams That Sell) *be set up and sized to cover the company's customers and target markets?*

START BY DECIDING WHAT YOU WANT YOUR SALES TEAMS TO SPECIALIZE IN

Deciding what you want your sales team to be responsible for is essentially about deciding what kind of specialization you want them to have.

- **Area sales teams** are set around customers that are geographically close to each other, and each sales team specializes in what is happening in that geographical area.

- **Industry sales teams** are set around customers that are in similar kinds of businesses, and each sales team specializes in different industry types.

- **Account sales teams** are set around customers that are similar in size, and each sales team specializes in managing different types of customer sizes (e.g., SMEs, large accounts, or key accounts)

For a long time, the most commonly chosen specialization for sales teams was that of being physically close to their customers, where each sales team would be assigned to cover a given geographical area and all the existing and potential customers within it would be covered by the sales individuals closest to each customer.

Geography and physical customer proximity is the dominant organizing principles for three reasons in particular:

- **Maximizes potential for physical visits by minimizing distance to customers:** With customers grouped together by geographical proximity to each other, the sales team is able to minimize time required for travelling between face-to-face customer visits and maximize customer-facing time (i.e., number and duration of sales meetings), that drives sales.

- **Maximizes potential for time allocation to customers and team cohesion by minimizing physical distance between team members:** With customers grouped together by physical proximity, the team members responsible for covering sales to these are also more likely physically closer to each other. This limits the time required for travelling whenever the team must meet, frees up more time for customers and creates a stronger team with more time together physically in an office.

- **Simple way to create nonoverlapping account portfolios that fit the Profit and Loss structure of business:** This structure ensures that all target customers are covered by a part of the salesforce while avoiding giving responsibility for sales for the same account to multiple sales teams or individuals. Dividing sales responsibility by geography is often in line with the company's existing organization structure and profit and loss (P&L) break down.

The closer salespeople are physically to the customer the better it is for sales performance.

The problem with having a sales organization whose specialty is to be physically close to its customers is that it there is a trade-off.

The closer you want sales physically to existing and potential customers that they are responsible for (increasing physical proximity), the broader an account type portfolio you typically need to give them (reducing customer focus and expertise).

> # The closer you want sales physically to existing and potential customers that they are responsible for, the broader an account type portfolio you typically need to give them.

While grouping together responsibilities for different types of customers based on their geographical location and proximity to each other may have made a lot of sense in the past, three major developments are forcing sales leaders to reconsider whether this still makes as much sense as it used to, for the following reasons:

1. **Less need for geographical proximity to increase sales efficiency:** With business-to-business buyers' growing preference for digital and remote interactions with their vendors, the share of physical interactions relative to remote ones declines and with it salespeople's need for physical customer proximity to reduce travel time does as well.

2. **Greater need for customer expertise to grow sales effectiveness:** With business-to-business buyers' growing use of digital channels and content for self-education and self-service, the need for salespeople to have deeper expertise in their customers' businesses and purchasing processes grows.

3. **Less need for physical proximity among sales team members:** Remote or hybrid work where people work from home more and less in office has become the new standard in many fields.

For sales leaders, this means they increasingly need to consider other characteristics of the company's target account profiles than geographical location when deciding on what kind of specialization they want to model their sales teams.

SPECIALIZE YOUR SALES TEAMS AROUND WHAT KIND OF EXPERTISE YOUR CUSTOMERS VALUE MOST

In a world where buyers are less dependent on salespeople to make simple transactional purchases (online or automated) and more empowered with an abundance of information to make more complex ones, salespeople need to become specialist advisors or risk becoming obsolete.

- Have the industry and solution insights to teach them about possibilities for improving their business

- Have sufficient expertise in the customers business to challenge them on existing ways of solving recognized problems or opportunities

- Have expertise in management of different stakeholder types to guide a diverse buying committee forward toward a shared buying vision and purchase

This is hard to do for different stakeholders at one specific customer type and close to impossible for generalist salespeople given responsibility for broad account portfolios of many different customer types.

Because buyers are becoming empowered to do more on their own, sales teams must up their games and find out how to bring unique value and guidance to customer interactions, and sales leaders must decide what kind of expertise they want to set their sales teams around.

- **Geographic specialization:** The team understands what is happening in the geographic market of the target customer and is able to teach them about the current trends in these markets (Germany, US, China, etc.).

- **Industry specialization:** The team has expertise in the industry of the target customer and able to teach them about current trends (pharma, FMCG, oil and gas, etc.).

- **Value chain specialization:** The team has expertise in specific parts of the industry or company value chain (sourcing, procurement, logistics, production, sales, finance, etc.).

- **Business type specialization:** The team has expertise in different business types along a business lifecycle (start-up, scale-up, SME, large enterprise, global enterprise, etc.).

- **Business customer journey:** the team has expertise with customers at different points along their development journey with vendors' companies (potential customer, new customer, lost customer, loyal customer, etc.)

- **Business ownership specialization:** The team has expertise in different types of businesses with different types of owners (private, listed, public, family, etc.)

The challenge for most sales leaders is that often all the above specializations are important, but they have to decide which is more important than the others to create sales teams around specific types of specialization.

If a company sells to companies of all sizes to six target industries in Germany and there are only room for six sales teams in Germany, what does the sales leader do?

- **Industry sales teams:** Create six industry sales teams, each covering the whole of Germany?

- **Generalist sales teams:** Create six geographical sales teams, each covering all industries but for smaller parts of the country?

- **Business development teams:** Create two sales teams responsible for new customer acquisition, two sales teams responsible for on-boarding and growing new customers, and two sales teams responsible for managing loyal key accounts?

- **Account management teams:** Create two sales teams responsible for small accounts, two sales teams responsible for medium-sized accounts, and two sales teams responsible for large accounts?

- **Hybrid (industry–geography) teams):** Create three sales teams covering two target industries each in Northern Germany and three sales teams covering two target industries each in Southern Germany?

The answer depends on the sales leader's assessment of the different types of specializations that the sales teams could be organized around and their relative importance for the sales effectiveness and efficiency of the company.

In other words, it depends less on *whether* the specialization matters (it almost always does in some way) and more about *what* matters the most, so the right prioritization can be made when deciding what sales teams should be organized around.

SALES TEAMS SPECIALIZATION

GEOGRAPHY (GENERALIST SALES TEAMS)

Key question	*Considerations*	*Important if*
How much does physical proximity to customers matter to sales?	How important is local knowledge to sales effectiveness?	Local knowledge critical to sell
	How big a share of customer interactions must be face-to-face?	High share of F2F interactions needed
	How big is the need for fast availability at customer sites?	High need for fast response time
	How concentrated or dispersed are the customers geographically?	High geographic dispersion

INDUSTRY (INDUSTRY SALES TEAMS)

Key question	*Considerations*	*Important if*
How much does expertise in customers' industries matter to sales?	How important is knowledge about customers' industries to sales effectiveness?	Highly important to sell
	How much does the knowledge required vary among targeted industries?	High variation
	How strongly and association do target customers have to their industry?	Strong association (we only buy from industry experts)

VALUE CHAIN SPECIALIZATION (FUNCTIONAL SALES TEAMS)

Key question	*Considerations*	*Important if*
How much does expertise in customers' value chain functions matter to sales?	How important is knowledge about specific value chain activities to sell?	Highly important to sell

	How much does knowledge required vary between value chain activities in scope?	High variation
	How strongly do target customers associate with operating in the specific part of the industry or company value chain?	Strong association (we only buy from marketing or sales experts)

BUSINESS TYPE SPECIALIZATION (BUSINESS SALES TEAMS)

Key question	*Considerations*	*Important if*
How much do size and growth matter to sales?	How much do target customers vary with regards to current and potential size?	High variation
	How much do target companies vary with regards to importance for company growth and revenue?	High variation

CUSTOMER JOURNEY SPECIALIZATION (CUSTOMER DEVELOPMENT SALES TEAMS)

Key question	*Considerations*	*Important if*
How much does the target customer's level of business engagement matter to sales?	How great is the need for clear division between customer acquisition and account development in sales?	Need for clear division of responsibility
	How well do our offerings lend themselves to a *land-and-expand* approach?	High fit
	How much do the needs of customers change with the level of use of our offering?	High change

Deciding what specialization you want your sales teams to have is essentially about deciding which smaller areas of responsibility to group together in teams by assessing the trade-offs between specializing more in one area at the expense of another.

Once you know what kind of expertise you want your sales teams to have, and what you are willing to give up to get it, the next questions are how many teams you need and how big each of these should be.

TO SPECIFY SALESFORCE SIZE REQUIREMENTS, DEFINE AND SEGMENT YOUR TARGET ACCOUNT PROFILE

To size a salesforce with regard to the number of teams and people in those teams, the first thing to do is to specify exactly who and what sales is responsible for, typically in terms of five characteristics:

- **Geography:** Where are the target customers that need sales coverage (e.g., continents, countries, regions, cities)?

- **Industry:** What kinds of businesses are the target customers in that need sales coverage (e.g., pharma, manufacturing, logistics, retail)?

- **Value chain specialization:** Where in the industry value chain does the target customer specialize (e.g., pharma R&D, pharma sourcing and distribution, pharma manufacturing, pharma sales and marketing)?

- **Size:** How big are the businesses of the target customers that need sales coverage (e.g., measured in number of employees, annual revenue, production units)?

- **Customer journey:** What part of the target customers' journey does needs sales coverage (e.g., no customers, new customers, existing customers)?

Although companies could certainly use more dimensions, and often do, (e.g., ownership structure, digital maturity, developments in key financials) to describe the specific customer types it targets, the five above-mentioned dimensions will typically suffice for the purpose of describing customer segments that need sales coverage.

	Question	Answer example
Geography	Where are the target customers located?	*Europe & North America*
Industry	What industries do the target customers operate in?	*Building & construction*
Value chain	Where in the industry value chain do the target customers operate?	*Building owners Professional house building companies Design and architecture companies Construction companies Building material dealers*
Size and growth	What are the business performance characteristics of the target customers?	*Companies with $500k– $5bn in annual revenue (all sizes)*
Customer journey	What part of the customer journey does sales need to cover?	*Targeting both existing customers and new potential customers*

*Table 4: **Account Characteristics.***

It is important to note that this is not an attempt to describe an ideal customer profile (ICP) for the company, but rather a target customer profile (TCP) that we need to ensure is being covered by sales in an ideal manner when we start organizing people around customers and deciding how many people are needed.

If all the target customers of a company were identical on the five above-mentioned characteristics, calculating the theoretical resource requirements in sales would be a straightforward task:

- Count the number of accounts that fit the target customer profile characteristics (e.g., 1000).

- Decide how much time should be allocated to each account to meet the defined sales targets (e.g., 2 days per account per year).

- Specify net selling time available per sales professional on the team (e.g., 250 days per year).

- Calculate sales professional FTE requirements (e.g., 1000 x 2 /250 = 8 sales professionals).

- Specify team member ratios (e.g., one customer success manager and one inside sales rep for every four sales professionals and one team leader for every eight FTEs).

- Size salesforce FTE and team requirements (e.g., 18 FTEs in total, split into two *Teams That Sell*, each consisting of one team leader, four sales professionals, two customer success managers, and two inside sales reps).

> From a salesforce design
> perspective, talking about
> an average customer is
> not meaningful because
> most companies work with
> different customer types.

The problem is of course that in reality, no two accounts are the same and salespeople need to differentiate between how much time they allocate to different accounts, because the expected pay-off from time invested will vary among them.

If a sales team of four sales professionals has responsibility for four large, key global accounts that account for 10% of total company sales, it might make sense to have the whole team focused only on selling to these four accounts (sales professional FTE requirements / account = 1).

For smaller accounts of existing -and potential customers a team of four sales professionals should be able to cover 4000 accounts (average sales FTE requirements = 0.001)

For most companies talking about an *average* customer is not a meaningful way to determine salesforce resource requirements because each customer they serve is unique.

SEGMENT YOUR TARGET ACCOUNT PROFILE TO MORE MEANINGFULLY ASSESS FTE SALES REQUIREMENTS

To calculate a more meaningful assessment of FTEs required in sales, the target account portfolio needs to be broken down into smaller segments that can vary regarding sales resource allocation.

- How does sales resource allocation vary regarding the size of the target company (i.e., segmenting into small, medium, large accounts)?

- How does sales resource allocation vary regarding the level of business engagement of the target company with the selling company (i.e., segmenting into prospects, new accounts, or key accounts)?

- How does sales resource allocation vary regarding the target company's kind of industry and company type in the industry's value chain (i.e., segmenting into different target customer types)?

- How does sales resource allocation vary regarding the target company's fit with its relevant ICP description?

The decisions in this bottom-up approach to the allocation of different levels of sales resources to target companies with different characteristics

are typically made based on an economic calculation meaningful allocation to different accounts from a sales and profitability perspective.

From an economic perspective it may not make sense to visit (i.e., allocate
in-person resources to) a small account more than once per year, because
the estimated pay-off from additional time allocation is lower than the
investment.

In the same way, it may not make sense to allocate an extra person to
a large key account team of four people, because the estimated marginal
return on this investment, measured as additional sales and profits, is not
worth the additional investment.

The example below shows a company where commercial leadership has
decided that sales resource allocation should vary among the target
customers in one of their industries regarding (a) the size of target
company, and (b) the potential to grow sales to the target company.

- **Table 1:** Decisions on the amount of sales resources to allocate to
  each account in the 25 different microsegments

- **Table 2:** Count of how many accounts exist in each of the
  microsegments within its total target market

- **Table 3:** Table 1 and 2 multiplied with each other to find that
  this specific company would need 34.65 FTEs in sales to cover
  their target market

TABLE 1: FTE allocation by account type						
	Plus 100m	1	0.8	0.6	0.4	0.1
	50 to 99m	0.6	0.6	0.6	0.6	0.6
COMPANY SIZE ($ revenue)	25 to 50m	0.1	0.05	0.05	0.03	0.01
	5 to 25m	0.03	0.01	0.005	0.001	0
	0 to 5m	0.001	0.001	0	0	0
		0%	25%	50%	75%	100%
		Potential growth sales (%)				

TABLE 2: Number of accounts in target market						
COMPANY SIZE ($ revenue)	Plus 100m	1	2	4	6	30
	50 to 99m	3	4	5	10	100
	25 to 50m	15	100	50	20	400
	5 to 25m	25	50	100	200	1000
	0 to 5m	100	200	300	500	10.000
		0%	25%	50%	75%	100%
		Potential growth sales (%)				

TABLE 3: Total FTE requirements						
COMPANY SIZE ($ revenue)	Plus 100m	1	1.6	2.4	2.4	3
	50 to 99m	1,8	2	2	3	10
	25 to 50m	1,5	5	2,5	0,6	4
	5 to 25m	0,75	0,5	0,5	0,2	0
	0 to 5m	0,1	0,2	0	0	0
		0%	25%	50%	75%	100%
		Potential growth sales (%)				

The bottom-up approach to salesforce sizing gives an overall idea about the total size required in a salesforce, sales division, or sales unit, and it also gives the sales leader an initial idea for different types of FTE groupings that can be managed by teams of 4–10 people led by a sales manager.

From the previous example, the sales leader in charge of creating sales teams of a meaningful size and joint focus could decide to create five sales teams:

- Bottom-right corner: One 8 FTE small-to-medium customer acquisition and growth team

- Bottom-left corner: One 8 FTE small-to-medium account management team

- Top right corner: Two 10 FTE large customer acquisition and growth teams

- Top-left corner: One 9 FTE key account management team

EXAMPLE: Total FTE requirements – 34.65						
	Plus 100m	1	1.6	2.4	2.4	3
	50 to 99m	1,8	2	2	3	10
COMPANY SIZE ($ revenue)	25 to 50m	1,5	5	2,5	0,6	4
	5 to 25m	0,75	0,5	0,5	0,2	0
	0 to 5m	0,1	0,2	0	0	0
		0%	25%	50%	75%	100%
		Potential growth sales (%)				

Although calculating the need for sales FTE resources to cover a defined market is the theoretically right way to size the salesforce, anyone who has ever worked in a company with P&L responsibility in sales will know that is rarely the way it really works.

In most cases, it's a matter of allocating an overall budget to sales and then figuring out how many resources can be hired from that to cover defined target markets or TCPs—in other words, a top-down approach to salesforce sizing.

THE MORE COMMON TOP-DOWN APPROACH TO SALESFORCE SIZING

The more common approach to salesforce sizing is the one linked to the company's budget allocation process:

- **Create budget:** Estimate expected sales (revenue) for coming year, coming from the different geographies and business areas the company operates in.

- **Decide on sales costs as a share of sales:** Decide on how much selling cost (excluding marketing), should account for as a percentage of sales (e.g., 15%), just as it is done for expected cost of goods sold (COGS) if the company does production. This number (selling cost / sales) will likely vary inside companies as well, depending on the level of investment expected in future growth. For maturing markets with higher growth, companies might allocate a higher percentage of sales as selling costs to invest in customer acquisition and growth. For mature markets with low or no growth, companies might allocate a lower percentage of sales as selling cost and capture a larger share as profit instead.

- **Allocate sales budgets to company business units:** Based on where sales are expected to come from (typically from a geographical and business unit perspective) and the desired investment in growth (percentage of expected sales allocated to cost of selling), the sales budget can be allocated to different business units, and part of that budget can go towards hiring FTEs in sales.

For example, if a large global life-science company ($1bn in annual revenue) is expecting 10% of its sales to come from MedTech sales in the DACH region and 15% of expected sales is allocated to selling cost, then 1.5% of total company-expected sales ($15m) for the year will be allocated to selling MedTech in region DACH and people can be hired out of this budget.

Although the process of budget allocation involves a lot of back-and-forth, it typically follows three steps to get in place:

BUDGET ALLOCATION PROCESS

Allocate business units' sales budgets to their different customer segments

Based on their relative importance within each company business unit (e.g., DACH MedTech), the budget is allocated among the different smaller segments within the business unit.

For example, if there are four subsegments in DACH MedTech sales (hospitals, clinics, dentists, and emergency response), and 50% of sales is expected from hospitals, then 50% of the sales budget for DACH MedTech ($15m x 50% = $7.5m) should be allocated to hospitals sales in DACH.

This budget could be further split into geographical segments for MedTech sales to hospitals in region DACH. If there are three markets in region DACH (Germany, Austria, and Switzerland), and 20% of sales and growth was expected to come from Switzerland, then 20% of the DACH MedTech budget for hospital sales (20% x $7,5m = $1,5m) would be allocated to Switzerland.

Size sales based on budget and estimated cost / sales FTE

This process is based on budget allocated to business unit subsegments (e.g., $1.5m allocated to MedTech sales to Swiss hospitals), and an estimated cost per sales FTE hired into the sales team covering the subsegment in question.

The cost per sales FTE hired into the sales team can of course vary greatly, depending on the kind of FTE required on the team. The price of an experienced sales executive primarily working through face-to-face customer visits is likely many times more costly than a junior inside sales rep, both in terms of monetary compensation (e.g., salary, bonus, benefits and stock-options) and other associated costs (e.g., transportation, F&B, accommodation).

This is one of the reasons sales teams with different types of profiles on the team, rather than just the same type of sales individuals, have the potential to increase sales efficiency, by using different people with different cost levels.

For example, if a MedTech sales executive in Switzerland would cost the company an expected $500k per year (including everything from salary and bonus to phone and travel), the company would be able to employ a sales team of three FTEs for MedTech sales to Swiss hospitals.

However, the same company might be able to get the same amount of work done with two sales executives and a sales supporter to take care of time consuming tasks not requiring customer face time, at a cost of only $100k per year, creating a sales efficiency improvement for the sales team as a whole (or the potential to hire more people to work on selling more).

Sum up the number of FTEs allocated to cover business units and their subsegments

Finally, to get the total number of FTEs budgeted to be employed in the company's sales functions, add up the number of FTEs expected in all the subsegments of the different business units receiving a budget allocation.

Regardless of whether a bottom-up approach, top-down approach, or a mix between the two is used to size the salesforce and create *Teams That Sell* around distinct target customer segments, the easiest way to calculate how many FTEs are needed is to first calculate it based on how many sales professionals would be needed to cover the target market if they were part of a *Teams That Sell*, and then add the complementary specialist roles need to join their team in the proportions that make sense (e.g., one Inside Sales rep per three technical sales professionals on the technical sales team).

While the top-down approach to deciding on the number of FTEs in sales is much more common for well-established companies, it fails to answer a key question in salesforce design, just as the bottom-up approach does:

> *How do I group together FTEs allocated to smaller segments, to create sales teams, larger sales units, and divisions in the optimal way?*

CUSTOMER CENTRICITY GUIDES HOW TEAMS ARE SET BUT NOT HOW THEY ARE GROUPED TOGETHER

When deciding on how to group smaller sales responsibilities together into sales team responsibilities (e.g., by geography and industry), the second decision is how to group these teams together into sales units (teams of sales teams), and sales divisions (groups of sales units).

Where the first decision on how to form sales teams around a specific type of customer specialization is made based on an assessment of what will best drive sales efficiency and effectiveness, the decision on how to create and form sales units and divisions is made with the selling company in mind:

- Sales teams are formed more with the customer in mind (customer centric, outside-in perspective) because sales teams are the operating units of the salesforce that engages with customers.

- Sales units and divisions are formed more with the selling company in mind (business centric, inside-out perspective), because sales units and divisions are business constructions made to guide strategy, resource allocation, and business accountability.

How sales leaders decide to group sales teams together into larger groups of teams depends mainly on the following three things:

- How big is the salesforce?

- How is P&L responsibility organized?

- Where is the sales strategy made?

1. THE IMPACT OF SALESFORCE SIZE ON SALESFORCE DESIGN

The larger the salesforce, the greater the need to create different levels in the sales organization to be managed by sales directors, VPs, or SVPs of ever larger areas of sale responsibility. Unlike the military, there are no set rules for how teams are grouped together into units, divisions, or battalions, but take note of the following good rules of thumb:

- A salesforce of a maximum eight sales teams can be managed by one global sales director, who is responsible for a sales unit. (A salesforce of approximately 60–100 people).

- A salesforce of a maximum 60–70 sales teams grouped under eight sales directors can be managed by one global VP of sales, responsible for approximately eight sales units (a salesforce of approximately 360 people).

- A salesforce of 360 sales teams grouped under eight SVPs and more than sixty sales directors can be managed by one global SVP of sales, who is responsible for approximately eight sales divisions (a salesforce of approximately 3,000 people).

This means that if the size of the global salesforce is no larger than 60–100 people in total under 6–10 teams, then the question of how to group together teams is a fairly easy one as it fits under 1 global sales director's responsibility.

If the size of the salesforce is above that, commercial leadership needs to decide on the type of specialization their "teams of teams" need to share, whether geography, target customer sizes, or industries.

2. THE IMPACT OF P&L RESPONSIBILITY ON SALESFORCE DESIGN

A golden rule of salesforce design is that those who are going to be held accountable for sales results should also have the responsibility for them.

In other words, those in the organization who are given responsibility for generating the sales that determine the potential size of the company's profits or losses should also be given the responsibility for managing the people in the sales organization that work to create that profit.

> Those who are going to be held accountable for sales results should also have the responsibility for them.

This means that if your company has organized business P&L responsibility into geographical markets such as countries and regions, then country market directors should be responsible for the sales teams in their areas and regional VPs should be responsible for groups of *Teams That Sell*.

The challenge, of course, is that some organizations work with matrixed P&L responsibilities where leaders of geographical areas, target customer industry segments, or company product types can all have P&L responsibility at the same time. So, if they are all held accountable for top-line results, who has the ultimate responsibility for deciding how sales should be best organized to deliver on this?

3. THE IMPACT OF WHERE THE SALES STRATEGY IS MADE

If it is unclear from the division of P&L accountability who should be made responsible for managing teams of sales teams, a good place to look is where the decisions about sales strategy are made.

Who decides which customer types to target, or how to allocate resources to new customer acquisition versus existing account development? Who chooses which parts of the company's offerings to push to different customer types?

Deciding where-to-play with the company's limited sales resources should connected with the responsibility for deciding how best to organize sales to win within those target customer segments.

In other words, if the decisions on how to allocate sales resources to different target customer segments is made at the regional level in a company, then the responsibility for salesforce design should also lie there.

DESIGN YOUR SALESFORCE WITH BOTH A BOTTOM-UP AND TOP-DOWN APPROACH

Deciding on how to size and group a salesforce into teams, units, and divisions is most often a compromise between what is ideal and what is practically possible.

A company might conclude from its target customer profile analysis that it would need forty sales professionals on ten sales teams to cover its target market the way it would ideally like to do so, but if it only has a sales budget of $1m, that is not practically possible.

This does not mean that salesforce sizing and design should only be approached from one angle or the other, but rather that most often the best approach is to solve the task from both perspectives.

- **Top-down:** Fixing a budget for sales may force it to narrow down the size of its TCP profile, so that it fits with how many sales resources they are actually able to use.

- **Bottom-up:** Analyzing the company target customer profile to understand it at a granular level may facilitate a decision by business leadership to allocate more of the budget to sales.

- **The compromise:** Using the bottom-up approach to inform decisions on how much sales budget should be allocated to grow sales with a given target customer segment and the top-down approach to shape prioritization decisions on who to target.

Regardless of how sales teams end up being sized, set, and grouped, one thing is for certain. Getting the sales organization *set* right is just the starting point.

Getting it to work right is where the real battle begins.

KEY TAKEAWAYS

- *Teams That Sell* use a helix-organization where value-creating units are separated from functional expertise, because *Teams That Sell* is essentially about doing away with professional functions as the dominant organizing principle for sales. Day-to-day operations happens in *Teams That Sell*, where different types of functional specialists are combined to conduct required selling activities. Specialist resources are hired and developed professionally in the functional specialist communities they belong to.

- The traditional way of organizing sales into teams was around geography and customers' physical proximity to each other, to maximize time for face-to-face visits. This is changing because buyers empowered to do more on their own demand a greater level of expertise from the salespeople they work with, and the increased adoption of digital and remote vendor engagement reduces the need for frequent in-person meetings.

- Instead of sales teams with generalist salespeople that cover smaller geographical areas, sales leaders increasingly decide to create sales teams with different types of customer specialization and expertise (e.g., industry, value chain, or business type specializations) and spread them out over a larger geographical area, because customer expertise is growing in importance and physical customer proximity is declining in importance.

- Sizing your salesforce from the bottom up follows five steps: (1) define your target customer profile to count the total number of accounts your salesforce need to cover, (2) break it down into smaller microsegments that will vary regarding an economically sensible number of sales resources allocations, (3) specify the sales resource investment required for accounts in each microsegment, (4) calculate sales professional FTE requirements for each microsegment given the number of accounts and sales resource investment requirements for each FTE, and (5) calculate the total salesforce FTE requirements with complementary members of the sales teams in the determined ratios that different types of specialists require.

- Based on this understanding, FTE requirements for each microsegment being covered, sales teams can be created by putting different microsegments together into teams of 6–10 people that can be managed by a team leader.

- While the bottom-up approach is the theoretically correct way of deciding on salesforce resource requirements, a top-down approach is also always taken, where a share of the company's total budget is allocated to selling and the size is ultimately determined by combining both the bottom-up and top-down perspectives.

KEY QUESTIONS FOR COMMERCIAL LEADERSHIP

- **What kind of specialization do you want your sales teams to have for the customers they serve?** How are customer requirements for expertise changing in your business? What kind of expertise would your target customers most value from the sales teams that work with them?

- **How much physical customer proximity are you willing to give up for higher customer specialization?** If customers increasingly place importance on expertise in their business, industry, or company type and less on physical proximity, how much of the latter are you willing to give up to increase the customer expertise of our sales teams?

- **What should be the theoretical size of your salesforce and how does this match with what you have today?** What are the characteristics of your target account profile and how many accounts are there? How many sales resources should you invest in different types of accounts (microsegments) that you serve? What is the gap between what you are investing in selling today versus what you should be investing theoretically

"The strength of the team is each individual member. The strength of each member is the team."

Phil Jackson

CHAPTER 4

HOW TO BUILD AND MANAGE TEAMS THAT SELL

Key takeaway:

Teams That Sell are set based on the specialist capabilities that are needed for the type of selling they need to succeed with. They are developed over time to perform and continuously exceed those performance targets.

Over the past decades, tech-behemoth Google has done more than use data to understand their users' motives and behaviors.

The company has become obsessed with understanding how to increase their own workers productivity, investing millions in research and measuring everything from how frequent people eat together to characteristics of their top performing managers.

In 2012, a new cross-disciplinary team of statisticians, psychologists, sociologists, and engineers was put together to answer a question at the heart of how the company was organized and worked:[52]

> *"What makes teams work?"*

---

52. What Google Learned From Its Quest to Build the Perfect Team - The New York Times (nytimes.com)

The standing belief in the executive layer was that great teams were built by combining great people who could get along:

- "It's better to put introverts together on one team and extroverts together on another..."

- "Teams are more effective when they are friends away from work..."

The only problem was that no one actually knew if any of this was true.

In Project Aristoteles, as the initiative was code-named (inspired by his famous quote "the whole is greater than the sum of its parts"[53]), researchers identified 180 teams to study (more than one-third of which were in fact teams in sales) and started collecting and analyzing data on their individual members.

But no matter how they arranged the data and looked at it from different angles, there were no patterns to be found (in fact, conclusions at times went in opposite directions).

> "We looked at 180 teams from all over the company... We had lots of data, but there was nothing showing that a mix of specific personality types or skills or backgrounds made any difference. The 'who' part of the equation didn't seem to matter."
> – *Abeer Dubey (Project Lead)*

The problem was, as the team would later find out, that what makes teams work is not generally related to the traits of its individual members.

It is about group dynamics and how team members work together.

It is about group dynamics and how team members work together.

---

53. re:Work (rework.withgoogle.com)

The study found that high-performing teams were characterized by five things:

1. **Psychological safety:** Psychological safety refers to an individual's perception of the consequences of taking an interpersonal risk or a belief that a team is safe for risk-taking in the face of being seen as ignorant, incompetent, negative, or disruptive. In a team with high psychological safety, teammates feel safe to take risks around their team members. They feel confident that no one on the team will embarrass or punish anyone else for admitting a mistake, asking a question, or offering a new idea.

   - *"If I make a mistake on our team, it is not held against me."*

2. **Dependability:** On dependable teams, members reliably complete quality work on time (vs. the opposite: shirking responsibilities).

   - *"When my teammates say they'll do something, they follow through with it."*

3. **Structure and clarity:** An individual's understanding of job expectations, the process for fulfilling these expectations, and the consequences of one's performance are important for team effectiveness. Goals can be set at the individual or group level, and must be specific, challenging, and attainable. Google often uses Objectives and Key Results (OKRs) to help set and communicate short- and long-term goals.

   - *"It's clear what we need to accomplish and we have well-defined structures for how we plan to do so."*

4. **Meaning:** Finding a sense of purpose in either the work itself or the output is important for team effectiveness. The meaning of work is personal and can vary (e.g., financial security, supporting

one's family, helping the team succeed, or self-expression for each individual).

- *"The work I do for our team is meaningful to me."*

5. **Impact:** The results of one's work, the subjective judgement that your work is making a difference, is important for teams. Seeing that one's work is contributing to the organization's goals can help reveal impact.

- *"I understand how our team's work contributes to the organization's goals."*

Project Aristoteles revealed to leaders an interesting fact about teams: the right group norms can raise collective intelligence of teams with average members, while the wrong group norms can do the opposite, even if its members excel on an individual level.

For sales organizations consisting of salespeople, who have spent the vast majority of their professional careers focused on individual performance optimization, it also poses a huge challenge:

> How do you get individuals to work together as a high-performing team?

TEAMS THAT SELL ARE SET BASED ON PEOPLE REQUIREMENTS BUT DEVELOPED OVER TIME TO PERFORM

Different types of *Teams That Sell* are set for different types of selling.

A technical sales team needs people with technical or commercial capabilities to complement the sales engineers on the team. A transactional sales team needs people with data and analytical capabilities to compliment the transactional sales reps on the team.

But as the research from Project Aristoteles reveals, setting the team with people who are the best specialists is not what determines whether the entire team will be successful.

The purpose of the team is to convert revenue potential into sales. This objective requires eight building blocks to be put in place to succeed within the specific customer segment that they are responsible for:

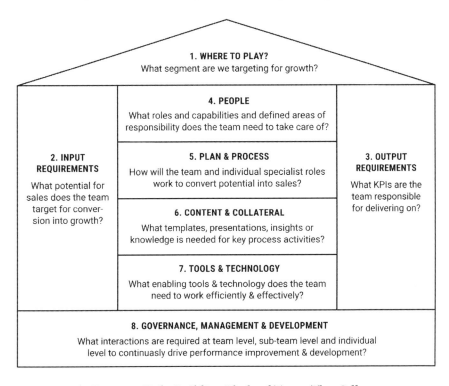

Figure 16: ***Eight Building Blocks of Teams That Sell.***
Elements to specify and put in place to have a fully operational Teams That Sell.

THE EIGHT BUILDING BLOCKS OF TEAMS THAT SELL

1. Where to play
Specify the target customer segments allocated to the team, with responsibility for growing business with these.

2. Input requirements
The team continuously identifies potential for sales to work on within the target customer segments they are responsible for.

3. Outcome requirements
The team consistently meets and exceeds business result targets and continuously demonstrates improvements through ongoing development.

4. People
Different team specialist roles are in place with clear responsibilities, the ability to conduct work, and high levels of interpersonal trust.

5. Plan and process
The team sets up, continuously executes, and improves systems of activities required to most effectively convert sales potential into revenue growth to grow performance over time.

6. Content and collateral
These elements include insights, content, and other types of sales collateral needed by the different customer-engaging roles on the *Teams That Sell*, such as challenger presentations for the team's sales professionals and digital content for virtual interactions for inside sales reps.

7. Supporting tools and technology
Technology enables the team to run their system of activities most efficiently and effectively, at both the team and specialist role levels.

8. Team Management Operating Model
The team leader drives performance from, and development of, team operations through a set of interactions taking place to a set frequency, at the team, specialist role, and individual team member levels.

Essentially these are the eight building blocks that are matured over time as the team is set and improved, following four stages of development for the *Teams That Sell*, toward high performance and continuous improvements.

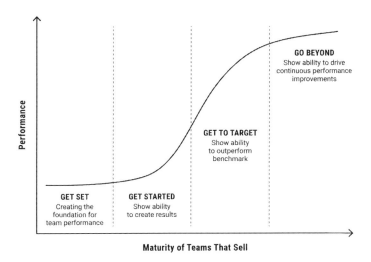

Figure 17: **Evolution of Teams That Sell.**
From getting set to continuously driving performance improvements.

1. **Get set:** Align the team around a shared understanding of purpose, goals, plan roles, and responsibilities while creating trust between team members (that they are now dependent on) regarding each person's ability to do their job well.

2. **Get started:** Show results on defined KPIs, although with lower sales efficiency and effectiveness, by getting the team to start executing on the minimum viable version of their system of activities.

3. **Get to target:** Show that the team is able to exceed the results that could be expected of a group of sales individuals by becoming continuously more efficient and effective at executing the team's system of activities.

4. **Go beyond:** Show that the team is able to demonstrate continuous performance improvement beyond their initial performance targets by continuing to make updates and changes to their system of activities and their use of supporting tools technology.

	Get set	Get started	Get to target	Go beyond
Team characteristics	*Need to clarify what to do, how to do it, and how to succeed together*	*Need to start operations to generate results, although still with low efficiency and effectiveness*	*Need to exceed sales and sales efficiency targets*	*Need to continuously evolve to demonstrate ongoing improvements to results generated*
1. Where to play	Team's customer target segment clearly defined	Team works with narrow target customer segment	Team works with full target customer segment	Team extends to test new adjacent target customer segments
2. Input	Team knows what sales potential to target and how to identify	Team starts activating defined sales potential sources to generate input for their system	Team continuously activates their defined sources of sales potential to generate required system input and meet their performance targets	Team explores new possible sources of sales potential to help them improve performance
3. Outcomes	Clarity on KPIs and role specific metrics	Initial sales produced, although with low efficiency and effectiveness	Team meets their performance targets	Team continues to improve performance indefinitely
4. People	Roles and responsibilities specified People with relevant capabilities hired Trust between team members in each person's ability to do their job	Growing proficiency in ability of specialist capability roles to practice in team's specific system of activities Trust in ability to depend on each other developed	Additional people within defined specialist roles being added to grow team's ability to perform Psychological safety in place for team to continuously try new things and dare to fail as part of learning	New complementary roles on the team tried and tested to explore new ways of increasing sales, efficiency and effectiveness from working as a team
5. Plan and process	Defined	Operational	Fully performing	Continuously changed to be improved

6. Content and collateral	Requirements defined	Content and assets for key interactions created	Content and collateral embedded in sales enablement platform supporting all customer interactions	Different content and collateral continuously tested for different situations for ongoing improvements
7. Supporting tools and tech	Defined	Minimal viable tech stack up and running	Full tech stack implemented	New ways of using technology to improve performance continuously explored
8. Management operating model	Interactions booked in calendar	Most essential interactions up and running	Full sales management operating model running	New ways explored for leaders to add more value to team performance and development

Table 5: **Team Characteristics at Different Development Stages for Teams That Sell.**

1) GET SET

Getting the team on the same page and specialist roles to define how to succeed

As Project Aristoteles and other studies have shown, trust between team members is key to team performance. But before focusing on building the kind of emotional trust that psychological safety falls under, there is a question that team members need to be enabled to answer first that is related to a different type of trust.

"Do I trust my team members, that my success is dependent on, to do their job?"

To answer that, the team of course first needs to have a shared and clear understanding of what exactly the team's job is, what success is and how they are dependent on each other to succeed.

The first step of the team leader is to get the team on the same page, with regards to four elements:

1. Purpose, goals, and objectives

2. Plan, roles and responsibilities

3. Mental models for success

4. Team leadership and operating model

GETTING THE TEAM ON THE SAME PAGE

1. PURPOSE, GOALS, AND OBJECTIVES

Key questions	Answer examples
Why are we here?	*We are here to help educational institutions and their students get more joy and impact out of learning by adopting new supporting tools for interactive teaching.*
How are you important to the business and your customers?	*We are responsible for growing the number of higher educational institutions in Canada using our solutions and growing how much they use it, to help more teachers deliver better learning outcomes and to help our company's ability to continuously invest in teaching development by bringing in new revenue.*
What is the vision you are working towards achieving?	*Our ambition is that all higher educational institutions in North America and all teachers there should be enabled by technology to deliver interactive teaching, rather than using old static remedies of chalk blackboards and projectors for one way communication.*
How will you measure yourselves on whether you are succeeding?	*Our goal is to* 1. *grow the number of educational institutions using our solution,* 2. *grow the average account value of institutions we work with, and* 3. *keep a high customer satisfaction rating from the continuous use of our solutions.*
What immediate objectives are you working toward achieving?	*The immediate goal for the year is to triple sales by (a) growing the number of customers from 100 today, to 200 and (b) growing the average annual purchasing from these from $10k to $15k, while (c) maintaining our current high customer satisfaction level.*

2. PLAN, ROLES, AND RESPONSIBILITIES

Key questions	Answer examples
How are we going to convert sales potential into sales?	*To succeed, we need to implement a system of activities to engage with our target account, that continuously* • *generate demand with relevant people in the educational institutions we target,* • *capture interest and nurture to initiate formal buying process ,*

* *guide interested potential customers through their decision process toward purchase,*

* *get new customers onboarded to start getting value from our solution, and*

* *expand business engagement and use of our solution with existing customers to grow value for them and sales for us.*

What roles is the team made up of and what is each role responsible for? What are the dependencies for success among the different roles?	*The team comprises five roles with complementary specialist capabilities in place to drive growth through new customer acquisition and account development:*

* *digital marketing specialist responsible for engagement with potential and existing customers through digital channels, to activate and drive forward buying processes,*

* *sales development rep, responsible for direct engagement with stakeholders in target accounts to identify and create new sales opportunities,*

* *AEs responsible for direct engagement with business decision makers to guide customer buying and development journeys,*

* *a customer success manager responsible for driving solution adoption in customer operations, and*

* *a team leader to plan, guide, and support the team's day-to-day work and ensure shared goal achievement through collaboration.*

3. MENTAL MODELS FOR SUCCESS

Key questions

Answer examples

How do we view our target customers and stakeholders?

There are three types of educational institutions we target, which vary regarding their primary driver for buying:

* *private institutions, concerned about their ability to stand out to attract private payer students,*

* *public institutions, concerned about their ability to demonstrate teaching impact and keep teaching staff engaged (avoid employee churn), and*

* *small independent institutions, concerned about their ability to continuously innovate on their teaching methods and approaches. Key decision-makers are institution deans, principles, or administrators with teachers as important influencers and mobilizers.*

What do we understand as important about how they buy?	*Better success rate when the buying process starts with the key decision-makers rather than the teachers. If it is not in the budget for the year, the money isn't found to buy during the year. Higher complexity classes like math or physics are optimal places for new customers to get started.*
What sales methodology do we subscribe to?	*We believe in the importance of challenging educational institutions on the existing way of teaching and enabling teachers to succeed in their roles. There is no burning platform for changing old blackboards to smart boards unless we create it by challenging them on their existing way of doing things and showing a way forward.*

4. TEAM LEADERSHIP AND OPERATING MODEL

Key questions	Answer examples
What role will the team leader play?	*The team leader has responsibility for helping the team as a whole and individual specialist roles on the team get clarity on what to do, how to do it and how to succeed together, while removing potential barriers to team success.*
What ongoing interactions exist between the team leader and the team, to guide work and goal achievement?	*This work happens predominantly through four types of interactions conducted by the team leader on an ongoing basis:*
What ongoing interactions exist among team members, to drive collaboration and alignment on a day-to-day basis?	• *team performance and development meetings,* • *sub-team coaching sessions,* • *one-to-one check-ins with individual team members and* • *weekly team check-ins.*

Although it is important that the answers to these questions are fully understood and bought into by the team, it is less of a *what do you think?* co-creation exercise by the team leader and more of a *here is the mission, plan, and approach as we see it right now, what is missing or needs further detailing?* approach.

The team is involved in the discussion, detailing and making adjustments, rather than co-creation to define the operating model from scratch.

Getting team members on the same page about purpose, goals, plan, roles, responsibilities and operating model, allows the team leader to succeed with two important things to get the team performing:

- **Get operating as a team quicker:** A quicker start reduces the risk that team members are working in diverging directions because of different perspectives about where the unit is heading and what is important, and on different operating models because of different ideas about the plan, roles, and responsibilities.

- **Get trust building started quicker:** Grow trust among team members so they know those around them are capable of taking on their designated roles and responsibilities based on their credentials.

Making sure that the team is aligned on their joint purpose, way of working, and individual roles and responsibilities enables the team to start working and develop initial trust in each other's credentials as functional specialists who get the job done.

Although it is the responsibility of the team leader to set direction, and the team of specialists to carry out the plan to drive growth, the team leader has a blind spot when it comes to the challenges that need to be addressed in the work of the team itself.

To specify challenges and solutions that makes the team work operationally, the team leader is dependent on the knowledge and skills of each specialist on the team.

GET SPECIALISTS TO SPECIFY HOW TO SUCCEED IN THEIR RESPECTIVE AREAS OF RESPONSIBILITY

Although the roles and responsibilities of each team member are clearly defined by the team leader, and based a plan for how these will overall work together to drive sales, the team is dependent on the specialist knowledge and skills of its different specialist roles to specify exactly how they their work is best conducted, what challenges need to be addressed to succeed, and what the solutions are to accomplish this goal.

As experts within their respective areas of responsibility, each type of specialist is responsible for identifying the answers to five questions that will influence how the team will operate and develop over time:

- **Activities:** How will work be conducted within the areas that you are responsible for to most effectively deliver the outcomes required?

- **Key success factors:** What will be the most important things to get right to succeed in a given area of responsibility?

- **Challenges:** What are the most important challenges to focus on addressing to get key success factors right?

- **Solutions:** What do you see as the solution to address defined challenges?

- **Dependencies:** Who else are you dependent on to succeed?

An example would be an inside sales rep on the technical sales team who has responsibility for lead management to convert interest into qualified sales opportunities for technical sales reps.

EXAMPLE. AN INSIDE SALES REP ON THE TECHNICAL SALES TEAM

Activities	Key success factor	Challenges	Solutions	Dependencies
Engage with new leads captured to qualify interest and ability to buy	*The ability to respond fast to incoming leads, as win-rates go down with longer lead response times*	*Potential capacity issues could cause slow response times during peak periods*	*Ensure automatic e-mail engagement is set up that comes personally from the Inside sales rep, as initial response to them reaching out*	*Marketing automation specialist to help set up personalized automation sequence for newly captured leads*
When a new lead comes in, we first categorize the lead to assess needs for direct engagement, to quickly call those assessed to be of high importance	*The ability to qualify leads based on criteria that maximizes win-rates and deal values for the team*	*Don't yet have the data to determine what characterizes leads that are most likely to convert to sales at a good average deal value*	*Set up lead characteristics data fields in CRM and get continuous feedback from AEs and from data on deals won*	*Data analyst to help with data gathering and analysis plus AEs to share feedback*
During the call we inquire about the customer's business, needs, and pains to qualify and create interest at the same time	*The ability to conduct initial conversations with different stakeholder types that not only qualify but also generate interest to set up account executives for success*	*Have to be able to conduct a "tailored" conversation with different types of stakeholders in different business types without having to spend a lot of time on lead research before reaching out*	*Develop call blueprints that fit different stakeholder and company types, based on best practice examples from other inside sales colleagues on other teams.*	*Insights from our conversation analysis tool about what works best in these types of conversations, for continuous improvement of call blueprints*
Qualified leads are handed over to leads through the CRM system, and e-mail introduction to lead and responsible account executive.	*The ability to handover qualified leads to account executives in a way that doesn't create a poor customer experience for the buyer*	*Handover from inside sales to AE could lead to poor experience for the customer if not managed well from the seller's side*	*Include AE in follow-up e-mail to customer and book meeting directly in their calendar, to avoid leads being left behind, from not being picked up by sales*	*Access AEs' calendars and acceptance of ability to book meetings directly in there.*

The team leader needs the team's functional specialists to not only carry out activities within their respective areas of responsibility based on what they see as best practice for the situation, but also to lead work on continuously addressing potential barriers holding them and the team back from success.

For the team leader, having the team's specialists develop their perspectives on how to succeed in their respective areas of responsibility serves three purposes:

1. **Establishes trust between team member roles:** By having the different specialist roles apply their professional skills to develop and share their perspective on how to succeed, other team members start to develop trust in their team members ability to do their jobs.

2. **Clarifies how to get team operations started:** Put together, the detailed areas of responsibility serve as the operating guide for each element of *Teams That Sell* and for the whole team, allowing the team to get started operationally.

3. **Clarifies dependencies:** Critical dependencies for success among different specialist roles are highlighted so agreement on points of collaboration among team members can make all the different parts work together.

The first two steps of team formation, after having set the *team to sell*, centers around aligning the team around what they have in common (getting on the same page), detailing how the different components will work and establishing initial mutual trust in team members' abilities to succeed together. It lays out the blueprint for how the team will operate together and individually to get the team off to the best start possible.

2) GET STARTED TO PERFORM AND BUILD TRUST IN OPERATIONS

Having agreed on the team's plan, roles, responsibilities, and operational details, and having established initial mutual trust regarding team members' abilities to do their part, the team leader is ready to put the team to work, to succeed with two things:

- **Show impact through a minimum viable system of activities:** Get the system of activities, carried out by the team's different specialist roles, started generating sales. This work does not yet have to be with high sales efficiency and effectiveness, but making a start will show that the team is capable of collaborating to generate results through an operating blueprint that can then be improved on over time.

- **Lay the foundation for a culture of psychological safety:** Get team members to develop psychological safety with each other and trust in their ability to depend on one another to follow through on their commitments. Take the level of trust from trusting people to do their job well to trusting the team's ability to collaborate and create impact.

It is in this early state of team development that the team leader's role and responsibilities within work planning, orchestration, and collaboration are of special importance to get the team operating, produce initial results, and grow trust. To expand on the foundational ideas just discussed:

SHOW IMPACT THROUGH A MINIMUM VIABLE SYSTEM OF ACTIVITIES

Like many other types of operational teams, *Teams That Sell* need to develop while performing and although the later phases of the team's development will be characterized by a higher focus on performance, when the teams operating model is up and running, the initial phases will be characterized by a higher focus on development than the initial impact they produce.

Get to the minimum viable versions of the team's system of activities to drive growth first, to demonstrate that it works, to start improving, and to show that it works better than the previous setup.

In cases where the team leader can borrow an already functioning setup from a similar team focused on the same type of selling but for another customer segment, this setup phase will be shorter, whereas teams starting from scratch will take longer to build the setup of activities that will best produce sales results.

Regardless of whether a *copy to tailor* or *build from scratch* approach is taken, this early-stage focus on building to start generating impact as quick as possible means that the team leader's role in the start resembles more that of a project manager than an operational manager.

To quickest lead the team's way to where they start demonstrating results, the team leader takes the following five steps:

FIVE STEPS OF CREATING A MINIMUM VIABLE SYSTEM OF ACTIVITIES

STEP 1: SPECIFY A MINIMUM VIABLE VERSION OF THE DESIRED END-STATE VISION

The leader agrees with team on the minimum viable version of the team's intended way of functioning to drive sales, based on the team's high level description of purpose, goals, operating blueprint, mental models, and detailed role-specific descriptions of each area of responsibility to make the team work.

This minimum viable version serves as the starting point for the team to start demonstrating results and start incremental development toward continuous performance improvement.

STEP 2: DEFINE DEVELOPMENT WORKSTREAMS FOR EACH SPECIALIST ROLE

The team leader arranges work building the minimum version of the team's desired operating model into separate development workstreams owned by the different specialist roles on the team, to be run in parallel. Because *Teams That Sell* consists of different components spanning marketing, sales, data and analytics, owned by different specialists on the team, each group of specialists is asked to define key activities and objectives on a timeline to get their part developed, with potential dependencies on other team members defined.

This gives the team leader a development plan that the team can execute in parallel and that can be used for on-going team meetings centered around development progress and barriers.

STEP 3: IMPLEMENT TEAM LEADER OPERATING MODEL

The team leader implements the on-going interactions among whole team, sub-teams, and individuals to a set frequency designed to drive forward development and performance improvements at the team, specialist role, and individual levels. These are the weekly team meetings, bi-weekly coaching sessions, and monthly performance and improvement meetings.

While the team leader will of course spend a lot of time addressing ad-hoc barriers to team development and performance, such as sorting out dependencies to other functions or addressing intra-team challenges, at least half the team leader's time should be spent on operating model activities.

Team leaders are their calendars and if they don't proactively take control of them with the on-going interactions they see as most important, other people will.

STEP 4: HIGH FREQUENCY TEAM MEETINGS FOCUSED ON DEVELOPMENT PROGRESS

The team leader sets up two types of ongoing meetings with the team members that take place once or multiple times per week.

A team meeting with all members participating, where progress status, next steps, and potential barriers are discussed *in plenum*, to ensure development alignment and progress at a team level.

The team leader meets with different specialist roles to help address potential barriers to progress on their specific workstream.

STEP 5: ACCEPT DEVIATIONS FROM TEAM'S FINAL OPERATING BLUEPRINT TO GET STARTED

Because development work on some workstreams may take longer than others, the team leader should consider whether some roles can get started operating before others are done with their development.

Although the intention of the team might be to have a digital marketing specialist take responsibility for lead generation and avoid having AEs spend time on this, the latter might already be able to start reaching out to stakeholders in the team's target accounts, and then transition out of this role as the marketing specialist is ready to take over.

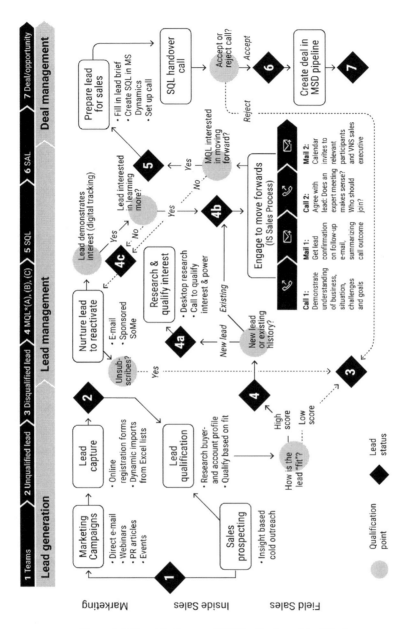

Figure 18: **How the System Will be Designed to Work.**
Example of a Teams That Sell system of activities to generate sales.

It is through this initial work building the team's system of activities, that the team starts working together to develop trust in each other's—and the team's—ability to follow through on their commitments.

It is also in this initial phase that the team leader starts laying the foundation for the kind of culture that is going to characterize the team and play a key part in how well the team performs.

FOSTERING A CULTURE OF PSYCHOLOGICAL SAFETY

The term "psychological safety" was coined by Harvard professor Amy Edmondson after her 1999 study[54] demonstrating how teams with better outcomes are more comfortable admitting mistakes, while teams with fewer good outcomes are more likely to hide their mistakes the term refers to team members' "belief that one will not be punished or humiliated for speaking up with ideas, questions, concerns, or mistakes, and the team is safe for interpersonal risk taking."[55]

Although each team member can and should do their part to promote this kind of culture, the responsibility to make sure it happens falls squarely on the team leader, and it is better done from the start than implemented with less success later.

Whole books have been written on the topic,[56], [57] but Amy Edmondson's 2014 TED talk[58] serves as a good starting point for team leaders to take action:

---

54. https://www.jstor.org/stable/2666999

55. https://psychsafety.co.uk/about-psychological-safety/

56. https://www.amazon.com/Fearless-Organization-Psychological-Workplace-Innovation/dp/1119477247/

57. https://www.amazon.com/Stages-Psychological-Safety-Inclusion-Innovation/dp/1523087684/

58. https://www.youtube.com/watch?v=LhoLuui9gX8

RESPONSIBILITIES OF A TEAM LEADER

FRAME THE WORK AS A LEARNING PROBLEM, NOT AN EXECUTION PROBLEM:

Although it is tempting to understand the team's initial problem as *not delivering sales*, it is more useful for team leaders to frame it is *not yet fully knowledgeable about how to operate to most effectively sell*.

It may seem like semantics, but this reframing of the problem as one related to learning allows the team to more easily focus on getting the problem solved, rather than focus on who to blame for the execution not working.

ACKNOWLEDGE YOUR OWN FALLIBILITY

Although the team leader is held to a high standard, and holds people on the team to the same, fear of making and admitting mistakes with the team leader seeps into the culture of the team.

At the core of Amy Edmondson's 1999 study about high performing teams is the openness about not being perfect and this starts with the team leader openly sharing with the team what they experience as challenging and sharing reflections on what they are focusing on improving.

The purpose of the team is not to become *perfect*, but to get into a state of *continuous improvement*, based on a willingness to admit fallibility.

MODEL CURIOSITY BY ASKING A LOT OF QUESTIONS

Although it is tempting for any leader to feel they are valuable by having all the answers, this is neither the intended role of the team leader nor how they best foster psychological safety. Especially because the team leader is not a functional specialist at the level of the people on their team, the role is more centered around asking the right questions.

What are the most important things that need to be done right to make this work? What are the critical challenges to address to get it done? What is the minimum viable version to get operational in your specific areas of responsibility? What concerns you the most about getting it done within the timeline we've agreed on? What support do you need?

A question-asking team leader accomplishes the facilitation of solution identification to progress team development and performance, while at the same time modelling the kind of curiosity desired within the team.

The team leader's responsibility fostering a team culture characterized by psychological safety is not something that happens alongside the team's work—it happens in every interaction that the team leader has with the team and the different specialist roles.

- Weekly team meetings focused on development progress and team KPIs are facilitated by the team leader as a team dialogue, rather than single-person broadcasting.

- Ongoing sessions between team leader and different specialist roles are driven by question-led coaching to help define key barriers to progress and identify solutions and next steps.

- Ad-hoc challenges for the team to progress development and performance are handled by the team leader with a *learning problem* approach, rather than a *whose fault is it* identification exercise.

The goals of this initial phase are to get the team operational, to start showing impact, to raise the team trust level, and to drive fast time-to-performance and continuous improvement beyond that.

Whether this phase is shorter for teams able to borrow elements from other similar teams that are already up-and-running, or longer for those who need to set up their system of activities from scratch, it needs to get done to get the team to the next phase of development where team operations are continuously improved on to continuously drive performance improvements.

3) GET TO TARGET AND 4) GO BEYOND: LEARN AND DEVELOP CONTINUOUSLY TO IMPROVE PERFORMANCE OVER TIME

After the initial phase focused on getting operational and getting team trust in place, the team should have accomplished the following five things:

1. **Team is able to operate:**
   The system of activities is set up, to be continuously executed based on the team's agreed *minimum viable version* of their desired end-state operating model.

2. **Team is operating:**
   The different specialist roles are conducting minimum viable version activities within their areas of responsibility to deliver the outcomes they are responsible for, and team members are collaborating where this is needed to make the team work as a whole.

3. **Team is delivering results:**
   The team has started to generate sales from running its system of activities, although likely not yet at the level of their KPI goals and with low sales efficiency and effectiveness.

4. **Team leader's operating model is running:**
   The team leader has implemented the team, sub-team, and 1-1 interactions taking place continuously and to a set frequency, to drive forward development and performance improvements.

5. **Team trust is continuing to develop:**
   The team is comfortable sharing and discussing areas for improvement and challenging each other to continue doing better.

The engine is running, performing, and moving forward, but perhaps still more like a first prototype of Gremlin than a formula 1 racer.

With the team's sales operating model set up, running, and generating initial results—although not with high efficiency and effectiveness—the team enters a new phase with its focus on continuous improvements to the way it works on an individual and team basis.

The team has shifted focus from primarily spending time developing the system of activities required to drive sales toward spending more time operating and continuously improving operations, to generate consistently increasing sales impact.

Less time and focus by team on building allows increased time and focus on performing.

For the team leader, this also means a change from a project manager role of a development team towards a team manager role of an operational *Teams That Sell*, with the following four important changes:

THE NEW TEAM MANAGER ROLE IN TEAMS THAT SELL

KPIS AND THEIR DRIVERS TAKES CENTER STAGE AT TEAM PERFORMANCE MEETINGS

Bi-weekly or monthly team performance and improvement meetings become centered around the team's KPIs and the metrics that drive them. The team looks at how the team is performing on its KPIs of sales, cost-of-sales, and changes since the last period and identifies the key challenges to be addressed by looking at the drivers of sales efficiency and effectiveness.

The purpose of these meetings is for the team to specify the key areas for improvement and actions to take over the next month to improve team outcomes and the efficiency by which they produce them.

Whereas the team leader initially used these meetings to discuss what needed to be developed to start performing, now the discussion centers on how the team is performing, to clarify where and how they need to develop.

FOCUS ON MAKING POINTS OF COLLABORATION WORK AT WEEKLY TEAM MEETINGS

Weekly team status meetings become centered around making sure the team's points of collaboration among different specialist roles are functioning, rather than focused on development alignment.

These weekly team meetings become less about making sure the team members are developing in the same direction and more about making sure the team operates in a mutually beneficial and aligned way.

The purpose of these meeting is to hear how everyone is doing and to discuss improvement potential and actions to take in the team's points of collaboration, as a proxy for the whole team's progress.

PERFORMANCE COACHING FOR CONTINUOUS IMPROVEMENT WITHIN EACH SPECIALIST ROLE

Bi-weekly or monthly meetings with each group of specialist roles on the team focused on their performance metrics and their drivers, identifying focus areas for improvement, barriers to address, and actions to take.

The purpose of these bi-weekly or monthly meetings at a team subgroup level is for the team leader to be updated on agreed-on actions from previous meetings and, through coaching, help the subgroup specify next actions to address identified barriers to better performance.

The valuable knowledge that the team leader brings into these sessions isn't expertise in the specialist role's domain, but rather an understanding of the team's entire system of activities and what development activities are going on in other specialist roles.

Although these coaching sessions are conducted directly with each of the team's specialist roles, and not at a team level, the team leader is able to ensure incremental development for performance improvement is still aligned for the team, even though this is no longer the primary focus of the team's joint meetings.

INVOLVEMENT OF CAPABILITY LEADERS FOR PROFESSIONAL DEVELOPMENT OF SPECIALISTS

Although the team leader should be perfectly capable of leading the team's operations and development to drive performance without possessing the same level of expertise as the specialist roles they are responsible for, there is one place where they fall short because of this inequality: observing the specialists in action to give feedback and coaching for professional skills improvement.

These 1-1 sessions are critical for the satisfaction, engagement, and professional development of the individual specialist on the team but are required to be done by the capability leader of the functional expertise team they also belong to.

The team leader must ensure that they are set up for their team members on an ongoing basis, in coordination with the functional leadership teams.

It is important to note that the shift is not made from one day to the next, but rather gradually, because the team's shift in focus and time from development to operations happens gradually.

As less time is allocated to development activities by the team, and more toward operational issues, the team leader's focus and activities with the team shift as well.

The team's goal is to move into an operating rhythm where results are not only achieved, but the team's system of activities and its individual members continuously develop to grow sales efficiency and effectiveness indefinitely, with the following five milestones to reach:

TEAM MILESTONES

TEAM OPERATIONS OUTPERFORMS SALES TARGETS

The first major milestone to achieve for a fully operational *Teams That Sell* is to collectively exceed the sales targets that could otherwise have been achieved by a group of individual sales reps or a factory setup of specialist groups regarding the sales they are able to generate and the cost they are able to incur.

TEAM CONTINUES TO IDENTIFY IMPROVEMENT POTENTIAL AND ACTIONS TO ADDRESS

Good *Teams That Sell* succeed with the initial milestone of outperforming sales and costs of sales targets. Great ones understand that there is no best-practice end destination for how they operate, and they continuously focus on learning problems that can be addressed to keep driving performance improvements as a key part of how they work as individuals and as a team.

TEAM MEMBERS ARE COMFORTABLE WITH CONSTRUCTIVE TENSION WITH HIGH WORK ENGAGEMENT

Good teams trust each other to be able to do their job and do their best. They want the best for each other and depend on each other. Great ones have the psychological safety in place to feel comfortable openly discussing potential for improvement and challenging each other to do better.

TEAM LEADER'S MANAGEMENT OPERATING MODEL INTERACTIONS ACCOUNT FOR 50% OF THEIR TIME

Although the initial phase of setting up the team to run its sales generating system of activities may have required a lot of the team leader's time for ad-hoc problem solving, once the team is up and running this should not be the case. The mechanism to ensure the team continuously performs and develops to improve performance is the team leader's ongoing interactions with the team, specialist sub-teams, and individuals. If most of their time is spent on ad-hoc firefighting, this critical mechanism is not functioning. Monthly team performance and improvement meetings, weekly team status and alignment meetings, bi-weekly sub-team coaching—managers are their calendars and need to proactively take control by booking in the ongoing interactions that serves as an operating rhythm for the team, to drive forward performance and development.

FUNCTIONAL CAPABILITY LEADERS INVOLVED IN TEAM MEMBER PROFESSIONAL DEVELOPMENT

The team leader will have ensured that functional capability leaders, related to the specialist roles on their team, conduct ongoing observation, coaching, and training for continuous professional development of individual team members and the transfer of new knowledge from other teams to theirs.

Although the team and its operations should by design be continuously evolving, there is one thing that should remain the same, to the extent that team members can set their clock to it, to make sure that this happens:

The team leader's management operating model.

TEAM LEADERS NEED TRANSFORMATIVE LEADERSHIP ON A BEDROCK OF TRANSACTIONAL LEADERSHIP

> "Great managers know and value the unique abilities and even the eccentricities of their employees, and they learn how best to integrate them into a coordinated plan of attack. This is the exact opposite of what great leaders do. Great leaders discover what is universal and capitalize on it."
> *HBR: What Great Managers Do (2005)*[59]

Google's 2012 Project Aristoteles wasn't the company's first venture into conducting extensive research into the people elements that make their organization work well. In fact, their research focused on answering what makes teams work was born out of work started four years earlier in 2008[60] that centered around using data to prove a different and more role-specific kind of hypothesis:

> *Managers don't matter and they don't impact team performance.*

The researchers found that managers *do matter* to team performance and that those that matter the most for team performance share 10 characteristics:

---

59. https://hbr.org/2005/03/what-great-managers-do

60. https://rework.withgoogle.com/guides/managers-identify-what-makes-a-great-manager/steps/learn-about-googles-manager-research/

1. Is a good coach

2. Empowers the team and does not micromanage

3. Creates an inclusive environment, showing concern for success and well-being

4. Is productive and results-oriented

5. Is a good communicator—listens and shares information

6. Supports career development and discusses performance

7. Has a clear vision or strategy for the team

8. Has key technical skills to help advise the team

9. Collaborates across the company

10. Is a strong decision-maker

Some of these characteristics are covered by design with *Teams That Sell* (e.g., empowering a team of specialist roles rather than micromanaging them), and some through the way that *Teams That Sell* are developed as covered in the previous section (e.g., having a clear vision or strategy for the team by getting on the same page or creating an inclusive environment through focus on trust building.

Where many of these manager traits need come into play is through the different types of interactions the team leader conducts with set frequencies at team, sub-team, and individual team member levels.

The team leader must be a good coach, listener, and information sharer in bi-weekly interactions with specialist roles to help them identify important areas for improvement, barriers to address, and actions to take to do so. They must be productive and results-oriented in monthly team performance and development meetings.

Collectively, we call these interactions the team leader's *management operating model*, which for *Teams That Sell* centers around the following six types of interactions:

	Interaction type	Frequency	Parti-cipants	Purpose
1	Team Strategy and planning	Low (1-2 times per year)	Team + sub-team	Evaluate performance of existing strategy and approach and agree on major changes to the team's *on-the-same page* statement and required developments to lift team performance
2	Personal feedback and development	Low to Med (quarterly)	1-1	Individual team members identify strengths to put in play more and areas of improvement to work on, related to how they work as a member on the team (not how they perform their own professional tasks)
3	Team Performance and development	Med (monthly)	Team	Identify team actions, changes, or developments required to either close performance gaps or improve on existing performance despite meeting requirements, and nurture team trust
4	Personal check-ins	Med (monthly)	1-1	Ensure team member feels safe, heard, and engaged in work on the team and identify actions required to address potential challenges
5	Sub-team performance & development		Sub-team	Help sub-team identify key barriers to address and actions to do so, to achieve and exceed performance targets and ensure development alignment with other sub-teams
6	Team status meetings	High (weekly)	Team	Ensure day-do-day team challenges at the operational level are discussed openly and addressed with a specific course of action

*Table 6: **The Team Leader's Management Operating Model.***

This is the team leader's operational backbone around all the ad-hoc problem solving that is sure to be part of the team's operations and development, to ensure that people are engaged in their work and trust each other, and that the team is operating and developing to perform.

1. **Strategy and planning:** Longer 1–2-day team and sub-team meetings taking place only once or twice per year, with the purpose of evaluating the performance of existing strategy and approach to agree on major changes to the team's *on-the-same page* statement and on what developments are required to lift team performance. Essentially this interaction is a team leader-led review by the team and sub-teams of the fundamental decisions that guide how the team is structured, operates, and develops to best deliver the outcomes they are responsible for.

2. **Personal feedback and development:** A 1–2 hour session with individual team members taking place 3-4 times per year, with the purpose of helping them identify actions to improve their ability to create value on the team, based on feedback from team leader observations and coaching. This interaction is about the standards individual team members are held to, given their experience, role, and responsibilities on the team and as a team member with shared responsibility for the whole.

3. **Team performance and development:** 1/2–full day team meeting taking place on a monthly basis, with the purpose of identifying potential actions in operations or development to lift overall team performance and to openly discuss potential intra-or inter-team challenges creating performance or trust issues. This is the interaction about the standards the team wants to be held accountable to, given what they and the team leader know that they should be capable of and about getting the team together to nurture interpersonal trust and build psychological safety.

4. **Personal check-ins:** 1–2 hour sessions with individual team members for the purpose of building interpersonal trust between

the team leader and the team member and to ensure that potential challenges at the individual level are surfaced and addressed on an ongoing basis.

5. **Sub-team performance and development:** 1–2-hour sessions with groups of team members that share the same professional expertise and specialization to help them perform and develop as a team within the team and with other team members. With each sub-group of specialists responsible for performance targets specific to their areas of responsibility, these are the interactions where the team leader helps the team identify the most important barriers to performance that need addressing and specify the actions required to do so.

6. **Team status meetings:** 1-hour team meeting, taking place with high frequency to ensure transparency around team performance, communicate relevant information, and ensure that potential team challenges are surfaced so they can subsequently be addressed.

The team leader should of course strive to be visionary, authentic, humble, inspirational, and all the other characteristics of a transformative leader, but the team needs to be supported by a bedrock of less sexy and unmodern transactional leadership interactions led by the team leader.

The big difference from traditional sales management, where the team leader is responsible for a group of similar individuals, is that whereas traditional sales management is predominantly centered around 1–1 interactions with individual group members that include professional (expertise) development, leading *Teams That Sell* is more heavy on team and sub-team interactions and leaves responsibility for professional development of individual experts to the functional capability leaders.

The team leader is an essential component of making *Teams That Sell* work, perhaps even more so than in traditional sales management, where individual members can be left alone as long as they meet their individual targets.

Leaders of *Teams That Sell* need to help both the individual members and the team as a whole perform and develop trust through operations and to lead team development that continuously improve performance over time.

The responsibility for making sure that team leaders are set up and equipped to succeed in this role falls squarely on the commercial leadership team as part of ongoing team leader training and as part of the first steps on the transition from teams of sales individuals to *Teams That Sell*.

Getting started on the transformation.

KEY TAKEAWAYS

- Although *Teams That Sell* are set based on the specialist capabilities required to make their specific type of selling work, the team's performance will not be determined by how skilled those individuals are at their specialty.

- Research from Google's Project Aristoteles showed that high-performing teams are characterized by

    1. high levels of psychological safety,

    2. high ability to depend on each other,

    3. high levels of structure and clarity on what to do and how to work,

    4. meaning in work, and

    5. high clarity on how the team creates impact.

- There are seven building blocks to get in place to have fully operational and performing *Teams That Sell*:

    1. Where-to-play decisions about the team's target customer segment,

    2. input for the team which acts as the potential they need to convert into sales,

    3. outcome requirements, acting as the performance KPIs of the team,

    4. people in place with the right capabilities and trust levels to perform,

    5. plan and process for the team to put into operations to convert sales potential into performance,

    6. tools and technology to enable the team to work with efficiency and effectiveness, and

7. a management operating model with team interactions in place to drive continuous development and performance improvements

- Team development happens through four phases, where the characteristics of the seven building blocks change through each phase:

    1. get set, where the team gets on the same page regarding their purpose, way of working, mental models for success, and trust in each other's ability to do their job well,

    2. getting started, where the team puts their system of activities into operation to start demonstrating results and develops trust in their ability to perform as a unit,

    3. getting to performance, where the team operates at full capacity to demonstrate their ability to meet and exceed their performance targets, and

    4. going beyond performance targets, where the team continuously tests, learns, and evolves to demonstrate continuous performance improvements.

- The team leader and their management operating model are at the heart of driving team performance and development through these phases. They schedule defined interactions that take place to a set frequency at the team, sub-team, and individual levels to ensure team operations function as intended and team development happens to drive continuous performance improvements.

KEY QUESTIONS FOR COMMERCIAL LEADERSHIP

- **What do the seven building blocks for your *Teams That Sell* look like?**
  How would you define their target customer segments, input and output requirements, people, plan, and technology?

- **How do you get the teams set?**
  What are the key questions that you want each team to answer, with regards to their purpose, objectives, and mental models? What is already given and what decisions are up to the team to decide?

- **Who should be team leaders and what should their management operating model look like?**
  Given the types of *Teams That Sell* that need to be developed, what kind of team leaders do you need? What interactions do you think will be critical for the team leader to implement in order for the team to succeed with performance and development?

"Not finance, not strategy, not technology. It is teamwork that remains the ultimate competitive advantage, both because it is so powerful and rare."

Patrick Lencioni

CHAPTER 5

HOW TO GET STARTED

Key takeaway

The journey toward *Teams That Sell* does not have to start, and should not start, as a large-scale transformation. It starts by showing that it works on a small scale, so that you can scale that out to the rest of the business afterwards.

If we want to start with why, the business case for commercial leaders to start transitioning from sales individuals to *Teams That Sell* is clear:

- Cost savings and sales efficiency gains, from more effective use of resources in the salesforce, by having highly paid specialists maximize the time they spend where they add the most value and on what only they can do

- Growth and sales effectiveness gains, by enabling customer-engaging people with responsibility for helping them buy, to spending more time with existing and potential customers and getting more out of this engagement

- Ability to scale by growing high-performing salespeople's abilities to cover larger account portfolios, by having a team that enables them to do more of what only they can do.

- Higher customer satisfaction from selling the way customers actually want to buy and higher employee engagement and retention by structuring work the way people actually want to work (i.e., in teams with a manager they trust)

Teams That Sell create a competitive advantage because it requires hard work to get.

The flip side of potential rewards is of course the investment requirements of realizing them and the associated risk. Despite clear rewards for commercial leaders that successfully cross the chasm from sales individuals to *Teams That Sell*, the journey does not come without its own set of risks.

IMPLEMENTING TEAMS THAT SELL—RISKS

Good salespeople leaving the company

Not everyone wants to be on a team and, perhaps especially true for salespeople working in an island setup, some prefer just to be left alone.

As with any meaningful but hard change initiative, changing the status quo comes with the risk that people performing well in their previous role cannot see themselves in the role envisioned for the future and leave as a result.

Although the risk of losing people you would have liked to keep can be mitigated with good change management and leadership practices, you shouldn't go on the journey toward *Teams That Sell* if you aren't prepared for it to happen.

Short term performance gaps for long term gains

Whenever we do change initiatives that involves new ways of working, we always expect performance to initially make a drop before bouncing back to a new and higher plateau resulting from the improvement, because it takes time and resources to learn new things.

Although the depth and duration people spend in the valley of subperformance can be shortened with good learning and development mechanisms, commercial leaders who aren't comfortable with short-term performance gaps to lift long term results should avoid transitioning to *Teams That Sell*, or any other transformative change initiative for that matter.

It won't work in our company

Although other companies have successfully transitioned from separated specialist groups to *Teams That Sell* and reaped the benefits of doing so, and the high-level business logic might make sense, many organizations' initial reaction to doing away with entrenched ways of working and replacing them with something new is the same.

We're different, it won't work in our company. The risk of people rejecting new ideas, strong reasoned as they may be, based on *it won't work here* is very real and prevalent, and commercial leaders not ready to show that it works and how it works before asking the broad organization to buy into it should be wary, or at least have very good communications and change management specialists onboard.

It may not work

As with all change initiatives there is always the risk that the idea was right, but the execution or timing was not.

For commercial leaders not prepared to risk failing, it is safer to stick with what no one is complaining about today.

For commercial leaders with the vision to take their organization to a new setup that helps them grow faster, lowers the cost of selling, scales better, and gets more engaged people, it is important to take these risks seriously and account for them in the transformation design.

Who can you get onboard first? Who will others follow after the first success? Where would you have least to lose with a short-term performance gap and stand most to win by showing performance improvements? How could you show the impact of a new way of selling in your company before asking more of the organization to believe in it as a way forward? How do you minimize the risk and cost of failure if it doesn't work?

The implementation of *Teams That Sell* creates a strategic competitive advantage for the companies that succeeds with it because it is hard, and because it is hard it also requires that they take a phased approach to succeeding with the change.

To manage the complexity of the transformation, minimize exposure to short-term performance gaps, and reduce the risk of *won't work here* resistance, the commercial leader in charge of the transformation should execute it in four phases:

1. **Prove it:** Select two pilot markets and prove the business case with two teams that share similar types of selling.

2. **Scale it:** Codify and expand the pilot market blueprint to additional markets with similar selling types.

3. **Expand it:** Expand the scope of the *team that sells* to other selling types, where new types of teams need to be set and developed.

4. **Develop it:** Unlike teams in sports, the game is constantly changing for sales and as it does the commercial leader needs to keep exploring new team composition types that best get the job done.

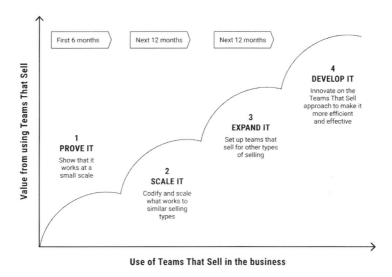

Figure 19: **Implementing Teams That Sell.**
From the first demonstration of how it works to its continual evolution over time.

Teams That Sell create better business results and a sustained competitive advantage for the companies that succeed with it, because it is a better way to solve the increasingly complex tasks of selling and more challenging to succeed with than the traditional salesforce setup of grouped sales individuals.

The way to manage the complexity of the transformation is to start small to successfully scale big.

START SMALL IN ORDER TO SCALE BIG

All transformations take their point of departure in similar claims:

- If we do X instead of Y, we believe we will be able to achieve Z.

- If we get marketing and sales to work together in operations instead of working in separate silos, we believe we will be able to reduce the total cost of selling while improving opportunity win-rates.

225

- If we get our sales managers to implement a sales management operating model that take up 40–50% of their time, instead of spending time selling and ad-hoc putting out fires, we believe we can improve sales performance and reduce employee churn rates.

These transformation claims most often come from what research has shown to work best in similar kinds of situations or what has worked well for similar company types.

Teams That Sell are no different. Although research shows that teams outperform groups of individuals for solving complex tasks (e.g., selling in the new buying environment), and we have concrete examples of other companies that have done it and seen business improvements from it, commercial leaders evaluating *Teams That Sell* as a potential transformation do not know for sure if -or how it will work in their organization.

For this reason, we advise commercial leaders to show how *Teams That Sell* work on a small scale in their specific business unit before making it a company-wide transformation, just as we would advise them with any transformation initiative that comes with high potential risks to operations and where a pilot approach is possible.

Prove the business case at a small scale in the company, before expanding it out on a large scale.

The first step on the journey towards using *Teams That Sell* on a company-wide scale starts with seven steps to learn how it works best in a specific company setting and to demonstrate that it works better than the old way of working.

SEVEN STEPS TOWARDS IMPLEMENTING TEAMS THAT SELL

STEP 1: DECIDE WHO HAS RESPONSIBILITY FOR THE PILOT INITIATIVE:

Although the transformation to *Teams That Sell* happens at the operational level of the business where selling is conducted, like many other development initiatives, it needs to be guided and supported by more centralized development resources with the knowledge, skills, and time required to drive change.

Global, regional, or market commercial excellence resources are typically the best positioned for this, with experience in both sales best practice and driving change initiatives toward it. T

hese are the people responsible for designing the initiative, enabling the pilot markets to run it, and conducting the final assessment on the pilot initiative, to ensure commercial leadership are enabled to decide on whether to scale it further out into the business.

STEP 2: SELECT PILOT MARKETS FOR TEAMS THAT SELL

Starting small means selecting 2-3 markets and customer segments, currently covered by sales individuals, where you want to test what a *team that sells* does to performance instead of a group of sales individuals.

These 2-3 pilot teams are preferably in different geographical areas to show that it works in more than one place; however, the places are ideally similar regarding the types of customers they are targeting and the type of selling they use to take their offerings to market.

This selection is done to first demonstrate how *Teams That Sell* impact performance for a specific type of selling in the company, while also showing that it works across geographies, to prepare for subsequent expansion of *Teams That Sell* into additional markets.

STEP 3: DEFINE THE TEST

The purpose of using *Teams That Sell* instead of a traditional group of sales individuals is to improve selling performance in terms of sales generated and cost of selling. To demonstrate this, a performance benchmark needs to be established for the traditional group of sales individuals that a *Teams That Sell* approach will be measured against. What does the new approach do to the teams' ability to create new sales opportunities, to the win-rate, and to customer satisfaction or employee engagement? Select the KPIs where you want to evaluate *Teams That Sell* and the benchmark numbers that will determine if the approach is successful.

STEP 4: SELECT AND ONBOARD PILOT TEAM LEADERS

Although all building blocks of the *Teams That Sell* are important (e.g., where-to-play decisions, input requirements, and plan and process), there is perhaps one piece that will be most important to get right, because the organization is dealing with something new: the team leaders—responsible for getting the team on the same page, getting them started, and getting them to performance targets.

These people should be hired primarily based on their ability to foster collaboration, potential, and willingness to lead the development and operations of a multidisciplinary team and, as research from the Peter Principle in sales shows,[61] not based on their previous performance at the frontlines of sales or marketing.

They should be onboarded to the purpose and ambition of *Teams That Sell* by the initiative owner and helped to recruit the members for the teams with the right capabilities required for their specific selling type.

STEP 5: SET THE TEAM AND GET THEM ON THE SAME PAGE

Depending on the type of selling the pilot market teams needs to succeed, different kinds of sales professionals and complementary roles will be required: sales engineers, inside sales reps, technical specialists, and content marketing specialists for technical *Teams That Sell*. Partner AEs, partner success managers, data analysts and playmakers, and partner marketing managers for partner *Teams That Sell*.

Ideally specialists for the teams are recruited from the existing internal specialist functions like sales, marketing, or inside sales, rather than hiring from the outside, because their existing knowledge of the company's offerings and target customers will help the team get to performance faster.

But, as we learned in the previous chapter, the team's performance will not be determined by whether the best individual specialists are hired, but rather by how good they will be at collaborating with others as one unit.

STEP 6: GET THEM STARTED AND GET THEM TO PERFORMANCE GOAL

With the team set and brought onto the same page by the team leader, as described in the previous chapter, the team leader moves on to the next phases of team formation and results creation. The leader will get the team operating as a team and continuously developing to improve performance through application of the team's management operating model.

Although the team leaders mainly need the support of the initiative owner and initiative sponsors in the commercial leadership team to gain access to the resources listed in step five, a more hands-on type of support and guidance is needed for this phase.

The initiative owner plays a key role in continuously helping the team leader manage team development, and the initiative sponsor in the commercial leadership team in helping the team leader through coaching and solving barriers to team success.

STEP 7: EVALUATE AND DECIDE ON NEXT STEPS

The final step is to evaluate the initiative from two perspectives:

1. whether the team's performance on the initiative's defined KPIs demonstrate a positive business case for conducting a company-wide transformation towards *Teams That Sell*, and

2. whether learnings have been gathered about what should be done differently to perform even better for the next wave of transformation.

61. https://www.kvadrant.dk/2022/04/26/promoting-your-best-salespeople-isnt-wrong-its-just-not-enough/

Starting small before scaling big serves four important purposes:

- It reduces the risk for commercial leadership of a change initiative hurting performance results that they are still responsible for generating through the current way of operating.

- It enables the commercial leadership team to make an informed decision about whether they see the business benefits of further investing in the journey towards *Teams That Sell* on a company-wide scale.

- It allows the commercial leadership team to learn how *Teams That Sell* works best in their company and use this trial run as the blueprint for further expansions into their business.

- It gives commercial leadership a strong case for change that they can use in their subsequent communication to the rest of the organization to rally the business around the new vision of how to set up selling. Instead of just taking their word for it, they can now use real life data from their own business as a more convincing reason for change.

This initial phase not only allows the commercial leadership team to make a more informed decision about whether they see that transformation make sense from a business perspective on a larger scale and see what their blueprint for *Teams That Sell* should look like, but also better sets them up for succeeding with the second phase of the transformation.

Scaling it.

SCALE TO SIMILAR SELLING TYPES FIRST, BEFORE EXPANDING OUT TO OTHER TYPES OF SELLING

After the pilot phase, the commercial leadership team should have accomplished two things:

1. They should have a business case for using *Teams That Sell* instead of groups of individual specialists, proven within their own company setting and based on performance of the pilot phase.

2. They should have a blueprint for what works best with a *Teams That Sell* approach for a specific type of selling within their company, based on learnings from the pilot phase.

While having these elements in place of course enables the commercial leadership team to better decide whether to invest more in the transformation and what to invest in developing, it also provides them with another critical element required to succeed with the transformation on a larger scale.

It gives them a clear change story to rally the organization around that contains five important answers to questions that people in every organization ask themselves when asked to do something different:

1. **Why do we need to change?** What is the burning platform for changing the way we are accustomed to doing things? What do we think we are going to gain from it?

2. **What are we changing toward?** What is the vision for the desired future state? What will it look like when we are there?

3. **What will the transformation mean for me?** How will my responsibilities, privileges, and power change with the transformation? Do I stand to lose or gain?

4. **What will I be required to be able to do?** What capabilities will I be required to have in this described future state? Do I feel

comfortable that I will be a success, knowing what I am capable of today?

5. **What will it require of me?** How much time and energy will I be required to put into making the change? Do I need to just work more to perform while developing?

Having good answers to these five questions matters for commercial leaders because these are the most commonly asked questions by the group of people in organizations who are both the most important to make the transformation a success, but also the most change resistant.[62] The sales managers.

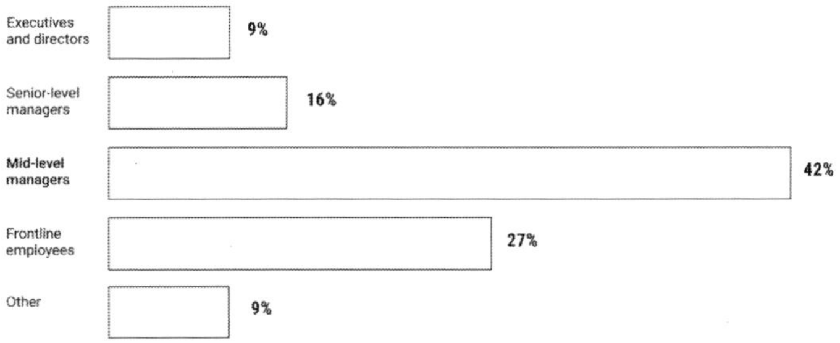

Executives and directors	9%
Senior-level managers	16%
Mid-level managers	42%
Frontline employees	27%
Other	9%

*Figure 20: **Who Resists Change the Most?***
Percentage of respondents, Prosci © change management study (2020)

To get management at the operational level onboard the change journey towards *Teams That Sell*, commercial leadership uses the business results, learnings, and operating blueprints from the pilot phase to communicate the change story to the organization.

---

62. https://www.prosci.com/blog/understanding-why-people-resist-change

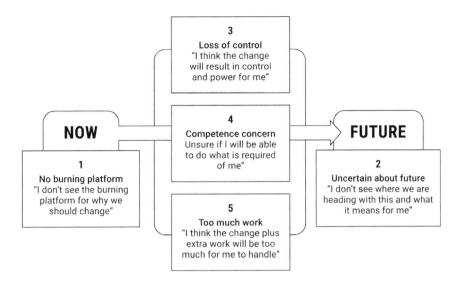

*Figure 21: **Barriers to Commercial Transformation.***
Five elements creating resistance to change in mid-level management.

1. **Use the pilot results to communicate about the burning platform for change:**
    For example, leaders might say, "Testing *Teams That Sell* in three pilot markets showed that using a combination of specialists on the same team, instead of our more commonly used setup of grouped individuals, created growth in sales, efficiency, and improved employee engagement."

2. **Use the blueprint of the pilot setup to communicate about vision for the future:**
    The leader could say, "Based on the results of what we did in the pilot, we will be working towards setting up our commercial organization to better succeed by having different types of specialists work closer to each other on teams and have each specialist maximize time on the tasks where they excel."

3. **Use learnings from the pilot phase to address concerns about loss of control, lack of competence, and being overworked:**
    The leader could say, "Besides positive business results, what we

could also see from the pilot was that people on the team were especially happy about having more time to spend on activities that fall within their professional areas of expertise where they feel most competent, by saving time on activities that they feel others on the team could do better."

Commercial leaders, responsible for continuously driving result improvements through change and people development, are no strangers to these types of change stories. But the difference in a change story based on hard evidence from the organization itself is the degree to which the people of the organization will buy into it.

Having a change story based on hard evidence and examples from their own organization increases transformation success because it better breaks down people's barriers to change and clarifies the need for the change, where they are heading, and how they are going to get there.

With the change story in place, commercial leadership has three options for how to proceed with the transformation and further scale out *Teams That Sell* in their organization:

1. **Scale to similar selling types:** Scale the blueprint from the pilot to other parts of the organization with a similar type of selling as in the pilot (e.g., to additional geographic markets within the same business unit).

2. **Expand *Teams That Sell* to new selling types:** Use learnings from the pilot to start creating *Teams That Sell* in parts of the business that have different selling types than were covered in the pilot (e.g., to same geographic markets as the pilot but in different business units).

3. **Do both at the same time:** Scale the *Teams That Sell* blueprint from the pilot markets to other markets with a similar selling type and start building *Teams That Sell* for parts of the business with different types of selling.

While it is tempting to use the pilot success to immediately start a company-wide sales transformation, the experienced commercial leader will know that one of the keys to successful transformations is to pick the lowest hanging fruit first and bite the change into smaller pieces.

Teams That Sell should first be scaled to parts of the organization with similar selling characteristics as the pilot markets for the following three reasons:

1. **It is easiest seen from transformation perspective,** because the blueprint from the pilot can be used with adjustments based on learnings.

2. **It is least risky seen from a business perspective,** because commercial leadership is investing in expanding something they have already seen work in one place to other, similar parts of the business.

3. **It is most effective seen from a people perspective,** because the change story from the pilot will best resonate there and address people's most typical barriers to change.

After scaling *Teams That Sell* to other parts of the business with similar selling characteristics as the pilot, commercial leadership can use the learnings from this initial expansion of their new way of selling when starting to transform the commercial organization in other parts of the business.

THE TRANSFORMATION IS OWNED BY THE BUSINESS BUT ENABLED BY COMMERCIAL EXCELLENCE

Most companies above a certain size have commercial excellence, or comex, functions to take responsibility for defining and running sales and marketing development initiatives to improve performance in the commercial organization.

Leaders define and implement best-practice selling processes for the company's different types of selling. They train people in the commercial organization to best run different key selling activities. They adopt new technology to best enable the commercial organization to do their work in the smartest way.

> ## Setting up teams for success requires the support of Comex functions.

Although the decision to restructure the organization's sales teams into *Teams That Sell*, rather than groups of individuals, falls under the commercial leadership team (CCO, business unit presidents, or marketing directors), development work to set up the teams for success most often requires the support of their commercial development function, for three reasons:

- **Lack of time and resources:** People in the business don't have the time available to manage larger change initiatives because they are busy in operations.

- **Lack of specialist knowledge in sales and marketing about best practice:** People in the business are good at doing what they are already doing now, but don't necessarily have the expertise or knowledge about what they should be doing differently to perform better.

- **Lack of specialist knowledge and change management expertise:** People in the business are experts in managing and operating the business, but not necessarily in how to best manage change to successfully transform it.

The people in the company's commercial excellence function typically use their specialist knowledge within sales, marketing, and change management to improve performance through decision-guidance and hands-on transformation support for business leadership within eight areas:

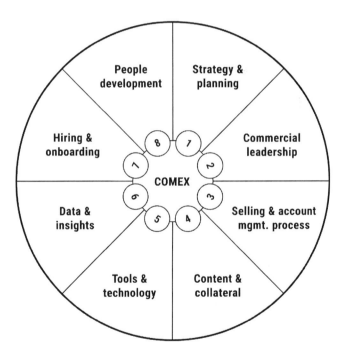

Figure 22: **The Eight Comex Elements.**
Enabling all levels of the commercial organizations to succeed.

EIGHT ELEMENTS OF COMMERCIAL EXCELLENCE (COMEX)

Strategy and planning: They enable business leadership to make right decisions about where to focus commercial resources (segmentation and targeting), how to size and organize the commercial organization and build compensation packages.

Commercial leadership: They help businesses recruit the right leaders in the commercial organization and set them up for success with the right management operating model and supporting tools in place to drive continuous performance achievement and development.

Selling and account management processes: They help businesses define and implement best practice selling processes, account management, and internal ways of working that fit their specific selling types.

Content and collateral: They help commercial organizations get sales enabling content, insights, and collateral in place, for use by the organization in different types of customer interactions with different types of customers on different types of channels for customer engagement.

Tools and technology: They help commercial organizations buy, implement, and adopt supporting tools and technology to help people in the organization work smarter and reduce time spent on activities that can be automated.

Data and intelligence: They help commercial organizations make better use of data about the markets they serve (i.e., their customers, people, and performance) for better decision-making at executive, managerial, and operational levels of the commercial organization.

Hiring and onboarding: They help commercial leaders and managers hire the right people for different roles in their organization and get them onboarded to start performing in their roles and places in the company.

People development: They equip different roles in the commercial organization with the knowledge and skills required to succeed in their roles, the company, and the selling environment they work in.

The observant reader will have noticed the similarities between the different elements that commercial excellence functions work to get in place and drive best-practices in general, and the eight building blocks that need to be put in place specifically for *Teams That Sell* (see chapter five). That is, of course, no coincidence, as the elements that commercial excellence functions work to put in place for their commercial organizations in general are the same when specifically applied to *Teams That Sell*.

Whether the commercial excellence function plays the role of advisor and guide or takes a more hands-on role in leading the transformation and taking responsibility for specific development activities, their expertise within sales, marketing, and change management is a valuable asset in making the transformation a success.

The commercial excellence function is essential in making the transformation a success.

KEY TAKEAWAYS

- *Teams That Sell* create business value and competitive advantage for those that make the journey, but like all meaningful change initiatives, it does not come without transformation risk.

- Both to mitigate transformation risks and improve commercial leadership's ability to succeed with the transformation, the preferred approach to manage the change is to start small, showing how *Teams That Sell* work in 2–3 pilot markets first, and scale what works to the company afterward.

- The pilot allows commercial leadership to better understand how *Teams That Sell* best work within their specific company and selling environment and how to create a more effective change story to use for engaging people more broadly in the commercial organization and bring them onboard with the transformation.

- *Teams That Sell* should first be scaled to parts of the business with a similar selling type as that of the pilot markets, rather than parts of the business with different selling characteristics, because that is where transformation risk is lowest and the change story from the pilot most effective.

- The commercial excellence function most often plays a key role in guiding, advising, and hands-on supporting the business in building effective *Teams That Sell* in the organization and driving the transformation.

KEY QUESTIONS FOR COMMERCIAL LEADERSHIP:

- **What are the ideal markets for you for pilot *Teams That Sell*?** Where would you stand most to gain by showing that *Teams That Sell* work, and suffer the least exposure to short-term declines in sales efficiency and effectiveness? Where would people in the commercial organization be most open to the transformation? Where would it be the most convincing to show results of a change story when scaling to other parts of the organization?

- **What transformation risks will be most important for you to proactively address?** What kind of resistance to change do you typically face when running commercial transformation initiatives? What barriers to change do you image would arise for a transformation initiative like *Teams That Sell* and which are most important for you to have mitigating actions for?

- **What specialist knowledge and skills within commercial transformation will be required to succeed?** How do you make the most of our internal commercial development resources to drive the transformation in the business?

FINAL REMARKS

Teams That Sell present a decision to be made by commercial leaders responsible for best setting up people in their organization to succeed:

Should they succeed as a business by focusing on how to get each person to succeed individually or by getting different specialists to work together in *Teams That Sell*?

In a company with a competitive and customer context that is continuously changing, the answer for how this change should be done is not a static one.

> The greatest things in business require hard work to get, otherwise they wouldn't be great to have.

Because a company's context is constantly changing, the organization must evolve as well, with two types of development initiatives to run:

1. Incremental development to the current way of work (with individuals working in separated functional silos), to achieve incremental performance improvements

2. Transformation of the way selling is set up, to reach a new plateau of salesforce efficiency and effectiveness

It is not that one is wrong, and another is right—all companies continue to succeed with their commercial efforts by doing both, but no one has ever won by never embarking on the second plan.

The transformative initiatives do away with old paradigms and mental models in the organization and replaces them with something that better serves the company in its new context to create a lasting impact on the business and the results it is able to generate.

Teams That Sell is just that.

Teams That Sell is a transformative initiative for the commercial organization that does away with optimizing sales efficiency and effectiveness at the level of the individual and instead looks at it from a team perspective.

As we have shown in this book, this transformation is not only needed in the new and more complex selling environment where commercial organizations find themselves, but also create superior business results through higher sales, lower costs of selling, a better customer experience, and higher employee engagement for the leaders making the transformation.

However, as with all the best things in business, *Teams That Sell* creates a competitive advantage not only because it is good for business, but also because it is a challenging transformation task to succeed with.

Because right decisions can still turn out wrong, because of poor change management practices and the application of these to the transformation initiatives, commercial leaders should take a structured approach to success and take one step at a time, starting small in order to scale big.

From teams of sales individuals to *Teams That Sell*—changing the way we sell one sales team at a time.

ABOUT THE AUTHORS

Martin Nyvang Mariussen
Partner, Kvadrant
Consulting

Thomas Børve Jørgensen
Managing Partner, Kvadrant
Consulting

Sixten Schultz
Partner, Kvadrant
Consulting

Martin Nyvang Mariussen has 10+ years of experience as manage-ment consultant to commercial B2B leaders with a special focus on commercial strategy, organizational design commercial transformation.

Thomas Børve Jørgensen has 15+ years of experience as a management consultant. He specializes in high complexity B2B sales and marketing and has led numerous global commercial transformation projects.

Sixten Schultz is an expert in B2B sales & marketing. With a strong background working in management consulting and in high-paced scale-ups. His focus in Kvadrant is on creating efficient and effective sales organizations.

INDEX

Made in the USA
Columbia, SC
07 May 2023

da298212-56bd-44bc-8b6a-db532756e3c1R02